THE STRUGGLE
FOR A SOUL

BOOKS BY WILLIAM L. HULL

The Fall and Rise of Israel
Israel—Key to Prophecy
The Struggle for a Soul

THE STRUGGLE FOR A SOUL

✠

WILLIAM L. HULL

Doubleday & Company, Inc.
Garden City, New York
1963

DEDICATION

To the memory of the millions who suffered and died, their deaths the results of Nazi lawlessness and hate, this book is humbly dedicated.

And I saw a new heaven and a new earth: for the first heaven and the first earth were passed away; and there was no more sea. And I John saw the holy city, new Jerusalem, coming down from God out of heaven, prepared as a bride adorned for her husband. And I heard a great voice out of heaven saying, Behold, the tabernacle of God is with men, and he will dwell with them, and they shall be his people, and God himself shall be with them, and be their God. And God shall wipe away all tears from their eyes; and there shall be no more death, neither sorrow, nor crying, neither shall there be any more pain: for the former things are passed away.

Revelation 21:1–4

APPRECIATION

Our thanks are expressed to those who assisted in arranging for our ministry to Adolf Eichmann—to Dr. Chaim Wardi, Counsellor to the Ministry of Religious Affairs, and to Dr. Z. Warhaftig, Minister of Religious Affairs in the Cabinet of Israel.

We are deeply appreciative of those of the police and prison officials who co-operated and who assisted us so willingly—of Mr. Behor Shitreet, the Minister of Police and Mr. A. Nir, Commissioner of Prisons, of the Warden and other officials at Ramleh Prison who were so friendly and co-operative, and above all of the Chief Warden of Ramleh Prison, who so patiently accompanied us during each visit to the death cell and freely proffered his assistance.

We would especially mention the invaluable assistance given to us by our friend, Mrs. Erna Stern, of Jerusalem, in aiding with the German translations. We are very grateful for her freely given help.

CONTENTS

FOREWORD

This is the story that never was told concerning Adolf Eichmann. The press of the world covered every stage of Eichmann's life from his childhood to his capture in Argentina, from his trial to his execution. From the time this writer's connection with Eichmann, as his spiritual adviser, was discovered, the world press frequently carried stories and pictures of our ministry. Yet the true story, the content of those conversations which took place in the death cell between the writer and Eichmann, was never disclosed to the press.

The question might be raised as to the propriety of revealing the content of conversations which took place between a man and his spiritual adviser. To some it would be considered unethical. This would have been so if our conversations had been on the level of the confessional, where priest and confessor are alone and the erring one reveals the secrets of his heart and life. Then I would have felt bound to respect the privacy of the man to whom I ministered, even an Adolf Eichmann. But such was not the case.

The security arrangements (Eichmann was one of the most closely guarded men of history) would not permit me to be in physical contact with the prisoner. We were never alone. Mrs. Hull was there and she, and never less than four police guards and the chief warden, heard every word that was spoken. There was even a strong possibility that tape recordings were being made, although this was later denied by the police.

As a matter of fact there was nothing confidential in anything that Eichmann said in our discussions, although much was revealed of interest from a psychological standpoint. I had not been called in to hear a confession. Eichmann told us that at the end he might say things privately to me if he could be with me without the guards. However, because of the need of maximum security right to the end and the brief time between the rejection of the appeal and the execution, there was no opportunity for me to be alone with Eichmann.

It should further be considered that this man was an unique human being who had once been a member of the Protestant church and then had turned himself into a monstrous assassin. The world is entitled to know, if it may be found out, how a living human being could yield himself to be used as such an awful instrument of destruction. The world is entitled to know, that it may be warned against itself, for it was the world that produced an Adolf Eichmann. If by a living "autopsy" on the mind of this man the source of the evil sickness could be discovered it was our duty to participate in the performing of this "autopsy" and to reveal its details to the world, so that a cure might be found and the disease eradicated. Only in this way can the terrible danger of the rising up of other Eichmanns be eliminated.

We had the opportunity of asking him many questions for which the world wanted answers. As his spiritual adviser, I would not deviate from the spiritual path, yet that context included many points of interest to psychologists and reporters and the answers are here recorded. In order to stir sympathetic chords, if possible, and to bring feelings of contrition and repentance, we spoke with the prisoner of his family, his own early life and church connections, his association with the Nazi Party, and subsequent events.

There were two reasons for my ministry. It began with the idea of justifying Israel's act in trying Eichmann and her complete fairness in doing so—even to supplying Christian spiritual counsel to the prisoner. It became imperative with the realization that the man came from a Protestant Christian background, and that he had a soul to be saved. Jesus

Christ had died for the soul of this man, too. *For God so loved the world, that he gave his only begotten Son, that whosoever believeth in him should not perish, but have everlasting life.* (John 3:16.)

The fact that Adolf Eichmann died denying any faith in Jesus Christ, any need of a mediator, was a tragedy, for no man on earth had greater need of a savior. But one faint ray of satisfaction emerges from the sordid picture—Adolf Eichmann's almost public rejection of Jesus Christ completely disassociated him and his evil deeds from Christianity. Christianity can be held responsible for producing an Eichmann, but not for his doing what he did. As the man in charge of finding a solution to the so-called "Jewish Question," he was completely separated at that time from Christianity and the teachings of Jesus Christ.

History will record the deeds of Adolf Eichmann for future generations. The record will not be complete without an acknowledgment that he had the opportunity, even unto the end, to repent and accept Jesus Christ as his Saviour. Those who read this book will be our judges as to the methods of approach we used and as to whether some other way or *modus operandi* might have been more effective in reaching the heart or in breaking down this man of stone. On the other hand, God alone can save. Salvation is not the result of winning an argument or of convincing someone of the *wisdom* of being saved. Salvation is the result of the gospel being preached to a heart tenderized and softened by the Holy Spirit. If such tenderizing and softening by the Holy Spirit is rejected and refused no mere words can save a soul. Salvation is through conviction and faith, the result of the Holy Spirit's work and its acceptance by the recipient.

Many will belittle our efforts to win the soul of Adolf Eichmann. Some will reject the gospel message we presented to him even as he did. They will judge him for his acts and condemn us for even suggesting that he could be saved. Some, not being sufficiently wise in spiritual things to realize that the Devil had blinded him, will rebuke us for not letting the man die in his supposed but false peace. Others will feel that they would have dealt with him in a different manner and would have been more successful. To all of these we can only say that we ministered to Eichmann to the best of our ability according to our own deep convictions and faith, accompanied by prayer. We have endeavored to honestly set forth just what was said between us, to give our words as we gave them, to translate Eichmann's thoughts exactly from the German. We did this to provide a historical record of the end days of his life. In writing after the event, changes could have been made in view of later developments, but we preferred to hold strictly to the actual day-by-day transcript of the proceedings so as to hand down this true chronicle of these conversations and our emotional reactions from day to day in the heat of the struggle for his soul.

William Lovell Hull

Jerusalem, June 1962.

SENTENCED TO DEATH

Chapter One ✠

It was 4:35 A.M. Friday morning, the first day of June,
1962. The rays of the hidden sun were pinking the sky to
the east as the ashes of Adolf Eichmann, one of the greatest
assassins of history, were slowly poured over the stern rail of
the Israel Police patrol boat *Yarden*. They fell into the foaming wake which plunged after the moving ship. For a moment the ashes were carried on the crest of the wave up
under the stern and then slowly sank into the churning
water. The disturbed water seemed symbolic of the unsettled
life now ended, which in its time had brought fear, suffering
and death to millions of Jews.

Slowly a weeping red orb rose above the bank of clouds
and then began to swiftly mount into the sky as the patrol
boat turned back to the misted shore more than six miles
away. In a short time we were back where the tender waited
to take us ashore to Jaffa Port, from where we had sailed only
an hour before.

My mind went back to twelve months ago, to my first connection with the Eichmann case. I had been a spectator, an
unofficial observer for the Protestant clergy, from the opening session of the trial. Over four hundred press correspondents had nearly filled the courtroom in Beit Haam, leaving

room for only a handful of the thousands who clamored for entrance.

The two most publicized trials in history had found their locale in Jerusalem. In both cases Jews and Gentiles were involved. The first, that of nearly two thousand years ago, involved a Jew, illegally seized by order of the Sanhedrin, then illegally judged, illegally sentenced, illegally slain by a Gentile court. More volumes have been published containing particulars of this trial than of any other in history. Here was innocency, a Man Who did nothing but good to mankind. He healed the sick and brought life to the dead. The greatest Man Who ever lived, but He was condemned to death by a Roman court.

And now—from the supreme height of righteousness we descend, two thousand years later, to the deepest depth of depravity and evil and gaze upon a man, a Gentile, being judged by a Jewish court. A small man, shifty-eyed, reputedly vile and wicked. We watch his eyes. In the courtroom only the rigidity of the man can be seen, whether standing at attention before his judges or seated with his hands folded. But we watch him on the closed circuit television in the press room. We see his eyes close up; they switch from side to side, around and around, almost as though seeking an escape from the glare of publicity and the awful revelations to come.

To mention the two prisoners in the same breath or to make comparison between them may seem blasphemous. Nevertheless, a consideration of the two trials and the contrast between them is of dramatic interest. The one was an illegal court, the Prisoner innocent but adjudged guilty. The second is a lawful, legally constituted court, the prisoner presumably guilty but up to the last moment clinging to the possibility of a verdict of "not guilty." A nation has been condemned for two thousand years as a result of the first trial. Some are fearful of what might develop from this second trial, that equal reproach might be the reaction, or even worse.

Without prejudging this man, who faces his judges charged with responsibility for the greatest deliberate slaughter of innocent people in the history of mankind, enough has been revealed and sworn to by witnesses in the Nuremberg trials and here to certify his complicity. No false witness at this trial, the facts are known and incontrovertible. Yet the most relevant witnesses cannot testify: they are dead, they were the victims—six million victims. The opening remarks of the prosecutor will rank with some of the great utterances of men. "Their blood cries to heaven," he dramatically declaimed, "but their voice is not heard. Thus it falls to me to be their mouthpiece."

In the early part of the trial the thin, sharp-featured prisoner with the black-rimmed glasses seems to pass out of the picture as the court and attorneys discuss points of law, the admissibility of letters, and other details. Indeed, the opening days of the trial reverse the situation, for the defense attorney questions the legality of the court and the laws of Israel to try the prisoner. Then the prisoner, through his attorney, becomes the accuser and the court the defendant until the beginning of the sixth session when the court effectively and completely maintains its competence to try the accused. There is almost a feeling of relief at the verdict, though no one could have expected any other.

The defense attorney claims that the prisoner was not in the circle of leaders. "The State," he claims, "should be charged and not the prisoner. The fact that Germany is paying reparations to Israel shows her acknowledgment of national guilt and responsibility. This man [Eichmann] was only a cog." Only a cog! As we gaze upon that shrunken man sitting in his chair we realize that he was only a cog, a tool. Not in him could be found the power and opportunity to slaughter millions of people. Only the might of the German nation behind him could put into operation such a diabolical plan—genocide. He was just a tool, but a willing tool. There is the guilt, there is the crime. A tool both *willing* to be used and even *desiring* to be used in the evil work.

There is something almost sacred about the proceedings. One could imagine that he was sitting in a modern church service, lacking only the organ and the singing. The trial seems to be lifted out of a mundane, worldly setting into the very heavenlies, as though God Himself is judging a guilty world which has produced such a monster as the prisoner at the bar—more than that and even worse than that, a guilty world which had stood unconcernedly and unprotestingly by while six million innocents suffered in agony —and died.

The words of the prosecutor seem inspired. His deliberate presentation of legal cases and facts defending the competence of the court causes impatience in some of the newsmen. Never mind; if they came to be entertained by a vulgar display of sensationalism, a Roman holiday, they deserve to be disappointed. Again, this is a sacred event which once more justifies the righteousness of God and the ultimate judgment of evil and evildoers. If there had not been a trial of Adolf Eichmann subsequent generations would either have emulated his acts or condemned this generation for cowardice and for sinking to the lowest ebb of morality.

There had to be a trial of this man and the machinery which empowered him. Only an acquiescent world could now stand by and consider the historic facts and withhold itself from judging the main instrument used for the awful crimes. If ever a trial by man was justified surely this is more so, and Israel has but led the way, not in a spirit of revenge but in fulfilling a sacred trust and obligation.

Can God forgive this man? If Adolf Eichmann is judged guilty by the court and sentenced to death he must die. Will death end it all? Tried by his fellow men and hung—will this expiate his crimes? No, this is not the end, this is not all that Adolf Eichmann has to face. True judgment must come to Eichmann after his death and it is this that he must fear more than the sentence passed in the specially prepared courtroom in Jerusalem. But if true repentance should come to this man would God forgive him? Is there forgiveness for such crimes? Can God forgive Adolf Eichmann? Here is the dividing line of decision over which man cannot and dare not step. He may sit in judgment on the acts of his fellow men. He may judge and even punish the evildoer with the death penalty. But he is not God. In the final analysis judgment is of the Lord. There at the last we must leave the soul of Adolf Eichmann, in the hands of God. God, Who alone is worthy to give the final judgment, will be his final judge.

The trial covered a period of four months from the first session to the end of the prosecution and defense attorneys' summing-up statements.

It cannot be said that the trial was of sustained dramatic interest. The Attorney-General, Mr. Hausner, was too thorough in the presentation of his case to cause constant tension in the listeners, and the frequent breaks for secondary translation slowed the proceedings. The presentation of a total of 1543 documents by the counsels inevitably produced long, tedious periods during which it was not unusual to see a press correspondent or an onlooker open-mouthed and sound asleep.

Yet there were many dramatic moments. There were times when the tension built up to a point where people burst out in shouts against a witness or the accused. One had to remember that the majority of the hundreds of onlookers at the trial were themselves survivors from Hitler's holocaust, or that they had lost their loved ones during that time. Justice Landau, the presiding judge, was very strict in dealing with any disturbance of any kind, such as laughter, which sometimes greeted the remarks of the accused as he testified, or talking among the audience; but on the few occasions when strong emotional outbursts occurred he was very kind.

There were other dramatic moments caused by the principals themselves. There was weeping as witnesses told of death marches, with young and old falling out and dying, faltering sick being shot and left as the plodding column moved on. The awful conditions existing in the concentration camps and the cruelty on every hand had double meaning for those who had gone through it and survived and now heard their story on the lips of fellow sufferers.

In the writer's estimation the two most dramatic moments were: One—the closing part of the films of the concentration camps shown in a closed-court session. To see the naked bodies tumbling over and over as they were shoved by a bulldozer into a deep pit did something to one which completely erased any feeling of pity one might have had for the man on trial. Two—the final cross-examination of the prisoner by the three judges, especially that of Judge Halevi. There were searching questions and tense moments here and especially when the judge put it straight to Eichmann and told him that this moment might be his last opportunity to tell the world the truth.

From a Christian standpoint several important facts evolved. Eichmann stated that his father had been a presbyter in the Evangelical Christian Church community. Yet when he (Eichmann) was given a New Testament to be sworn at the beginning of his testimony he said, "I do not swear by the Bible. I swear by Almighty God, because I am not bound by any confession, but I do believe in God." Again, he testified that twice he snatched a New Testament from his wife's hands and tore it up.

This had been my clue to Adolf Eichmann's background. His father had been of the Evangelical Church; without doubt Eichmann had been brought up in a true Christian atmosphere.

A man with such a background might even yet be reached by the gospel, in spite of his rejection of the Bible. Old chords might vibrate again, childhood memories might restore faith; and early teachings revived might bring confession and repentance for the awful deeds he had done.

Above all I realized—although I could find no feelings of compassion for the man in the bulletproof glass cage—that he was a human being and as such he had a soul. According to Christian doctrine and the words of Jesus Himself, Jesus had died for his soul as much as for mine. Even the soul of an

Adolf Eichmann could be saved if he would believe in the Lord Jesus Christ as his Saviour.

Early in the trial I determined that I should advise the Ministry of Religious Affairs that from Israel's standpoint it would be advisable to appoint a Protestant spiritual adviser to Eichmann. The trial was being handled in such a scrupulously correct and fair manner that no opening should be left for criticism from any part of the world. A Protestant spiritual adviser would forestall criticism from certain sections of the Christian world, and especially if the verdict of the court should be death.

In May 1961 I broached the suggestion to Dr. Chaim Wardi, Counsellor of the Ministry. Discussions followed with Dr. Cahane, the Director of the Ministry and Dr. Warhaftig, the Minister of Religious Affairs. It was felt that the matter was not one of immediate urgency. Eichmann for the time being was taken up entirely with his defense and the many documents involved in the case. He was not yet found guilty.

The trial was completed and the court adjourned. Four months passed and on the eleventh of December the court again assembled, now to pronounce the judgment.

"I open the one hundred and twenty-first session of the trial. The accused will rise." Thus Justice Landau, the presiding judge, began the closing day of the trial. Expounding his reasons and answers to arguments of prosecutor and defense attorney he came to his closing statement with these words:

"This court sentences Adolf Eichmann to death for the crimes against the Jewish people, the crimes against humanity, and the war crimes of which he has been found guilty."

In a marathon reading feat of five sessions, three of them on the first day and lasting until 9 P.M., the three judges in turn had read out their reasoned judgment. During all of it Eichmann sat somewhat detached as though having only an academic interest in the case. He scarcely moved, sitting by the hour gazing at the judges as though he were more interested in the legal aspect and in hearing how they arrived at their conclusions than in the decision itself.

And now Adolf Eichmann awaits death. His appeal has yet to be heard by the five Supreme Court judges. It is very doubtful that any decision will be given contrary to that of the trial court. It is less likely that the President will interfere to show clemency to the accused.

After twenty months of imprisonment since his capture, and one hundred and twenty-one court sessions, Eichmann must be in a condition of mind where he realizes that nothing but a miracle can prolong his life. How can he look for mercy? Did he ever show mercy? There are many who are opposed to his execution—why? He has been given the fairest of trials; he has been found guilty based upon irrefutable evidence. On the basis of legality what other sentence can be given? His crimes were illegal—his trial legal and just.

Shall we then feel compassion for the man? To us who have watched him through the long months of the trial there was little in the appearance or words of the man to move to pity. He seemed to have no pity for himself, unless it could be indicated by his words which he spoke in answer to the judgment: "I am not the monster I am made out to be. . . . It is my profound conviction that I must suffer for the acts of others. I must carry the burden imposed upon me by fate." These were his last words in court.

Whether "fate" had any part in it, we cannot know. This we do know: that the word of God tells us that *the soul that sinneth, it shall die*. Adolf Eichmann has heard his earthly judgment but his final judgment is yet before him. The awful solemnity of a court of law passing the death sentence on a man can be nothing to the solemnity of standing before God, unprepared, and hearing His words of judgment— *Depart from Me*.

Until now Adolf Eichmann has not asked for a spiritual adviser. It is conceivable that he will maintain this rigid attitude until the last.

SPIRITUAL ADVISER

Chapter Two ✠

On the twenty-second of December, 1961, I wrote to the Commissioner of Prisons as follows:

Mr. A. Nir,
Commissioner of Prisons,
Tel Aviv, Israel.

Sir,

In view of the verdict and sentence now handed down to the German Nazi war criminal, Adolf Eichmann, it would seem incumbent upon the State of Israel to offer a spiritual adviser to its prisoner.

Eichmann testified that he holds to no particular religion or sect. His father, however, he explained to the court was an evangelical Christian, which would mean a Christian of fundamental faith. Presumably Adolf Eichmann was brought up as a child in the circle of his father's religion.

The writer is of the evangelical fundamental Christian faith and upon the recommendation of the Ministry of Religious Affairs was selected to unofficially represent the Protestant Christian clergy at the Eichmann trial. As such I attended the majority of the sessions.

Whether the convicted prisoner appeals his case or not I believe that he should, at this time, be offered the opportunity of spiritual consultation with a Christian clergyman. As such I offer my services at your convenience.

Sincerely yours,

William L. Hull

On the twenty-third of January, Mr. Nir replied that Adolf Eichmann did not wish to have me visit him.

I wondered what approach had actually been made to Eichmann. I felt that possibly he had not been very encouraged to have a clergyman visit him, for the prison authorities would not be anxious to have the security of their prisoner endangered.

Dr. Servatius, the defense attorney, had made an appeal to the Supreme Court against the judgment and the sentence passed by the Jerusalem District Court. Due to his illness some delay was permitted before the presenting of his brief.

I decided to put on some pressure and arranged an interview with Dr. Dov Joseph, the Minister of Justice. He was not very receptive to the idea of my visiting Eichmann.

"He said that he did not want to see you, that's it," was Dr. Joseph's summary of the situation. He continued to say, "Eichmann is a grown man; if he wanted a minister he could ask for one."

I expressed some doubt as to whether the matter had been fully presented to Eichmann. Dr. Joseph suggested that if I felt that way I should have Dr. Servatius inquire from Eichmann.

"He will be back soon for the appeal hearing," Dr. Joseph said. "Why don't you see him and have him discuss the matter with his client."

Shortly after this it was reported in the press that Dr. Servatius was back in Jerusalem. I made an appointment for the fifteenth of March to see him at the King David Hotel.

Dr. Servatius was very friendly. I explained what had

happened up to now and expressed the thought that Eichmann should have a clergyman at this stage.

"I discussed the matter with him some months ago," Dr.
Servatius replied, "and he told me that he did not want a
spiritual adviser. However, he also said that if he did have
someone he would prefer a Jesuit priest; he felt that he would
understand his position better than anyone else."

Dr. Servatius added that Mrs. Eichmann and her children
were Roman Catholics, but that Eichmann had no thought
of converting to Roman Catholicism if he should see a priest.
He said that it was difficult to talk with Eichmann heart to
heart because of the glass separating them and the necessity
of talking through microphones and headphones. He explained that the prison guards listened in to every word that
was spoken. Eichmann had admitted that he was morally
responsible and guilty, but Dr. Servatius claimed that because of the security arrangements he could not discuss this
aspect of the case with him.

"I will be seeing Eichmann tomorrow," said Dr. Servatius,
"and I will ask him whether he wishes to see you."

The next day Dr. Servatius telephoned me after his visit
to Eichmann in Ramleh Prison. "Eichmann would *like* to
see you," he said.

This was the answer then. It opened the door. I telephoned
Dr. Joseph's office and was instructed to contact the police
officer in charge at Beit Haam when the appeal hearing
would begin. Eichmann had already been transferred from
Ramleh Prison to Beit Haam, and the hearing began the next
day, Thursday, the twenty-second of March.

On the opening day of the appeal I approached Lt. Col.
Leo Koppel, the police officer in charge at Beit Haam. I had
known him from the trial sessions and he was very friendly.
I informed him that Eichmann had told Dr. Servatius that
he would like to see me as a spiritual adviser and that Dr.
Joseph had suggested that I contact him (Mr. Koppel) to
make arrangements for me to do so.

Mr. Koppel said that he would arrange for me to see Eichmann after he had been returned to Ramleh Prison. He explained that the arrangements at Beit Haam were not convenient for interviews. Later, as the appeal hearings drew to a close on the twenty-ninth of March, Mr. Koppel told me that he would see Mr. Nir, the Commissioner of Prisons, on the first of April and suggested that I telephone Mr. Nir in Tel Aviv after he had contacted him.

Dr. Servatius had seen Eichmann again after the close of the appeal hearing and he telephoned me before leaving on his return to Germany.

"Eichmann," Dr. Servatius said, "told me that he was serious about the matter of your visits and reminded me that he had asked for you to visit him. He said that he would be *glad* to see you."

Dr. Wardi telephoned a message that Dr. Warhaftig (Minister of Religious Affairs) had spoken with Mr. Shitreet (Minister of Police) recommending me in the capacity of spiritual adviser to Adolf Eichmann. Dr. Warhaftig assumed that there would be no further difficulties in my making arrangements to see Eichmann.

In order to arrange all details of our ministry an appointment was made for the eighth of April to visit Mr. Nir at his office in Hakirya, Tel Aviv.

At this meeting I explained the steps that I had taken in the matter and the results which followed.

I told Mr. Nir that I had two requests to make in regards to arrangements:

One, that I should visit Eichmann twice every week until the end or until he was released.

Two, that Mrs. Hull should accompany me as interpreter.

Mr. Nir was not enthusiastic about our visiting him immediately. He suggested that Eichmann's appeal might succeed or that the President might grant clemency. "There would be time enough," Mr. Nir said, "when it is established that Eichmann must die and he knows it."

He was not sure whether it could be arranged for me to see him as often as twice a week, and he felt that Ramleh

Prison was not a fit place for Mrs. Hull to visit. This was the prison where the worst cases in Israel were detained; no women would visit there. The police would provide an interpreter.

My reply was that it was not a question of one or two visits. It was not a case of being sent for to hear a confession or to give last rites. Our ministry to Eichmann would be an attempt to convert him, to bring him to an active faith in Jesus Christ. It was not conceivable that with such a character as this conversion could be accomplished (if at all) in one or two visits. On the other hand, if we waited for the final decision, the execution might follow so soon that we would have no opportunity at all. (As a matter of fact this is what did happen; we could see him only for a short visit during the last hour of his life, following the President's rejection of his plea for clemency.)

We pointed out that it was necessary for us to see him at least twice a week beginning at once in order to have time to properly instruct Eichmann.

In regard to Mrs. Hull accompanying me, I explained that she was my co-worker in the gospel work and that only she could properly interpret my thoughts on spiritual matters. A Jewish policeman would not understand what I was talking about and much of the effect would be lost.

Mr. Nir suggested that I write a letter setting forth my requests and reasons for same. This looked as though it might be suggested as a means of evading the matter or delaying it for some considerable time.

I replied somewhat heatedly that it was twelve months since the subject first had been broached to the government, and that if I had to start writing further letters now Eichmann would be hanged before I could see him.

"It is only one week," Mr. Nir replied, "since I first heard that Eichmann had expressed a desire to see you. This letter will be handled at once; there will be no delay."

Paper was brought and I wrote a letter in longhand addressed to Mr. Nir who stated that it would be placed immediately before the highest authorities and that his secretary, Mrs. Epstein, would telephone to me in Jerusalem within a day or two and inform us of the decision.

Two days later Mrs. Epstein telephoned to say that it had been arranged for Mrs. Hull and me to visit Eichmann at Ramleh Prison at ten the next morning, Wednesday, the eleventh of April. We were to bring our identity cards to identify ourselves. Further visits would be arranged on each Sunday and Wednesday, but I should telephone Mr. Nir's office the day before each visit to ensure that arrangements had been made.

Thus began a ministry which lasted for exactly fifty days.

AT RAMLEH PRISON

Chapter Three ✠

My wife and I had prepared a series of studies in logical progression on man and salvation, under eight headings. These were:

1. God's judgment versus man's.
2. All have sinned.
3. All are lost because of sin.
4. Christ died for sinners.
5. All can be saved.
6. Salvation is through faith.
7. Faith is a gift of God.
8. Jesus is coming again—resurrection of dead and living.

We proposed to deal with each subject in a series of Bible studies. Our objective was first to bring to Eichmann a sense of guilt for his deeds of the past—then a realization of his lost condition, spiritually—then the revelation that through Jesus Christ his sins, even all his vile deeds, would be forgiven.

In the event we never were able to bring him to an unqualified realization of his personal guilt before God. If we had been successful in the first point we probably would have succeeded in the other two. But it seemed that through the years Eichmann had so schooled himself in thinking he was justified in everything he had done that by the time he was brought to trial his mind was firmly set.

There was a space of fifteen years after the war, prior to his capture, in which he had ample time to consider his defense, to rationalize his excuses, to justify his acts. More than that, he was in prison almost a year after his capture before his case came to trial. That year was spent in intensive study, in reading on points of law, in studying the charges of the prosecution, in examining and finding answers to the hundreds of incriminating documents, letters, etc., which bore his signature. In Jelameh Prison, where he was held prior to his trial, he had shelves of books and documents which he consulted and studied.

If he had been charged at the time of Nuremberg or shortly after the war ended and we had had a similar opportunity to minister to him, we might have been able to bring him to admit his guilt. In 1962, seventeen years after the war ended, we probably faced a very different Eichmann from that of the year 1945.

Though we had a number of friends among the press of Israel and foreign press correspondents we decided that nothing should be made known of our visits to Ramleh Prison for the time being. However, we did invite some of our Christian friends to pray with us for the success of this mission. We realized that in taking on this task we would, in a sense, come face to face with the Devil himself. We realized that the power of Satan was tremendous and that in our own strength we would be helpless. Yet here was a human being with a living soul, in spite of what many might say. Jesus Christ died for his soul and we felt it our duty to make known to him that *God so loved the world, that he gave his only begotten Son, that whosoever believeth in him should not perish, but have everlasting life.* "Whosoever," I believe, must include even an Adolf Eichmann.

Ramleh Prison is thirty-five or forty miles from Jerusalem. For more than half the distance one travels the winding road through the Mountains of Judea. We had driven this road many times in the twenty-seven years of our residence in Jerusalem, but never before on such a desperate mission.

Our appointment was at 10 A.M. We arrived at the outer gate of the prison ten minutes before the hour and gave our names to the guard. Two minutes later a prison official came out from the prison and escorted us to the main building. It was always the same officer who conducted us on this part of our visit, and we enjoyed his friendly greetings and our short conversations as we walked from the gate to the warden's office and then back again at the close of each interview. In time he became a real ally and supporter. When one of the Hebrew papers objected to our visiting Eichmann and I wrote a letter to the paper, he stoutly maintained the rightness of our position.

As we waited in front of the prison for the heavy iron door to be unlocked on our first visit, I began from then to count the number of locked doors and gates we must pass through. We had already waited at the gate and been passed through the two locks there. The heavy door of the main building swung open and we were led through the corridor to the office of the warden. His door also was locked.

We received a very friendly greeting; indeed, everyone was very polite and cordial in their welcome to us. They showed no resentment to our disturbing their maximum security arrangements.

The chief warden was responsible for Eichmann. He had sole charge of the prisoner under the commissioner of prisons and gave all his time to this one prisoner. Protection against a double danger was required. There was the danger that an effort might be made to harm Eichmann, or conversely that an attempt might be made to rescue him. Damascus and Cairo were full of ex-Nazis employed by the Arabs in their hate campaign against Israel, and the possibility of an attempted helicopter landing on the roof of the prison was not ruled out.

The warden invited us to sit down and discuss our visit.

Coffee was served. It was explained to us that we would not be searched, but we were asked to leave anything in our pockets in a locked cupboard. We were rather surprised. We had expected a thorough search to be made. They explained that if they had thought it necessary to search us we would not have been allowed to see Eichmann. I told them that I had brought a German Bible with me and that I wanted it to be given to Eichmann. I handed the book to the chief warden, who gave it a brief examination. I explained that I wanted Eichmann to keep this Bible in his cell so that he could study it and that it will be available each time we visit him. The chief warden said that he would give it to Eichmann during our present visit. It would then be taken and thoroughly examined by "security," and given to Eichmann in his cell. I said that that would be agreeable to me. We had a duplicate German Bible for Mrs. Hull so that we could give him the page number and save the time required for him to find a scripture reference.

Word was brought in by a prison official that all was ready, so, escorted by the chief warden, we left for Eichmann's cell to begin our desperate battle for the soul of this man. To begin with it was a duty mission rather than a visit of compassion and mercy, but as time went on I struggled against a God-given feeling of pity and affection for the soul of Adolf Eichmann.

Leaving the warden's office we went down the hall and turned to the right and out a door in the back of the building. Again turning right we came to an iron door in a concrete wall. A tap on the door was answered by the uncovering of a four-inch slot from the inside. After we were inspected by the guard inside, the door was opened and we entered. This was a small, walled courtyard, about ten feet by twenty-five feet in size, open to the sky. We walked the length of it to another iron door, this one leading back into the main building. Here, after inspection through the panel opening, the key was handed by the guard in the courtyard to the guard inside. The door could be opened only from the inside, but the key was held by the outside guard.

Entering through the door we climbed three flights of stairs to the third floor. It was a private stairway, inaccessible from the rest of the building. We were accompanied up the stairs to the third floor by the guard who carried the key for the upstairs door. Again the small panel door opened for inspection, and on instructions from the chief warden accompanying us the guard handed a key to the man inside and the iron door was swung open.

We now entered the death-cell apartment, but a locked iron grille had yet to be opened before we could come into the death cell proper. Altogether there were eight locked doors to be passed, seven of them of solid iron or iron gratings. A ninth iron grating locked the prisoner into his inner cell.

The actual apartment had four separate rooms, one in each corner. Coming in from the stair landing one usually found two or three, or even more, guards standing in front of a large screen which hid the left hand part of the apartment. Later I found that behind this was the kitchen, where all meals were prepared. This was in the left hand corner, and opposite, with a space between, was the room used by the chief warden as an office and staff room.

None of the guards or prison officials in this death-cell apartment were armed. They had neither guns, clubs, nor weapons of any kind. They were locked in and could not get out until a key was handed them from outside the door. All partook of the same meals, including the prisoner, so that there was no chance of his food being poisoned.

While we waited the final lock was turned and we entered through this opening on our right. Inside on the left was a wall with a gray blanket pinned up covering the iron grating leading into the room in which Eichmann was held. For interviews with his attorney, Dr. Servatius, and now for us, the right hand side of this first room had been walled off. It made a small cubicle about six feet by twelve feet. This room was divided in half by a wallboard partition, from wall to wall and three and a half feet high, and from the wallboard up by bulletproof glass. There was a small shelf from wall to wall on each side of the separating glass and wall, with a microphone and earphones on each shelf. The door at the far end by which the prisoner entered his part of the cubicle was an iron grating. On our side was a plain wooden door. On the outside a covered balcony ran across the front of the whole apartment. The front of this balcony had been bricked up leaving two long, narrow openings for air. The window which had opened onto the balcony in the end of the cubicle used by the prisoner was now used by a guard who stood on the balcony and leaned over the window sill of the open window.

THE FIRST VISIT

Chapter Four ✠

Wednesday, 11th of April

Eichmann was already in his part of the cubicle when the chief warden ushered us into our part. He rose as we entered, bowed, and remained standing until we were seated on the two chairs provided for us. We smiled at him.

In addition to the guard at Eichmann's window there was another one by the locked iron grating door and one by our door. The chief warden usually stood in our doorway or nearby. This was the minimum force within view. There were additional guards outside the cubicle as well as in the part of the death cell apartment which we had first entered.

Eichmann, for this first meeting, was dressed in a business suit, with white shirt and tie. They were the same clothes that he had worn during the trial and appeal. He was now seated a distance of two or three feet in front of us with the glass separating us. He looked much thinner at this close range than our view of him in the court. His face was very pale, almost bloodless, his eyes were light blue, the pupils very large. The chief warden went into Eichmann's part and placed the German Bible we had given him at Eichmann's right hand.

We settled ourselves, put on our earphones, and then I leaned forward and spoke into the microphone.

HULL: *Guten Tag.*

EICHMANN: *Guten Tag.*

HULL: Do you understand English at all?

EICHMANN: (shook his head)

HULL: (translated by Mrs. Hull) My wife will translate, then, into German.

EICHMANN: (nodded)

HULL: We have come to help you.

EICHMANN: Dr. Servatius told me that you had come to him and expressed a desire to talk with me. I knew that you would be coming, but did not know when. I would like to know what you believe, of what faith you belong.

HULL: I am an evangelical Protestant. Your father, I believe, was of a similar faith. (Eichmann did not seem to respond in any way to the mention of his father.)

EICHMANN: I have not made a deep study of the Bible, but I have read it. I wish to make myself clear in the beginning. I know God; I have never lost touch with God. (We were shocked by his statement. He continued on but I interrupted because we were not given much time at first and I wanted to leave some thoughts with him for him to consider.)

HULL: We cannot take time now for you to do a lot of talking; our time is limited. (In court, when Eichmann was questioned, the presiding judge had great difficulty in restraining him from long dissertations and in getting simple answers to questions.)

EICHMANN: Can I discuss these things later?

HULL: Yes, later you will be given an opportunity to talk. Now we have come to read the Bible and to discuss it with you. Today we want to talk about God's judgment in contrast with man's judgment. There is a judgment of God to be faced. Please turn to Luke 12:4-5. (We had given him a list of scriptures which formed the basis of the first day's approach. See Appendix.)

EICHMANN: (With some hesitation he found the page number we gave him and tried to read. He had on his distance glasses and found it difficult to read so Mrs. Hull read to him from her German Bible.)

MRS. HULL: *I say unto you my friends, Be not afraid of them that kill the body, and after that have no more that they can do. But I will forewarn you whom ye shall fear: Fear Him, which after he hath killed hath power to cast into hell; yea, I say unto you, Fear Him.*

HULL: I want you to notice the two judgments here—man's and God's. It is God's judgment which should be feared. You have had man's judgment, but you have yet to face God's judgment.

EICHMANN: My God is too great to bother with the little things of man.

HULL: Every person, good or bad, has to face God and be judged for the good or bad done here. Now please turn to Ecclesiastes 12:14.

EICHMANN: Is that in the Old Testament?

HULL: Yes.

EICHMANN: I will not read the Old Testament; it is nothing but Jewish stories and fables. I refuse to read them.

HULL: (firmly) The Old Testament is the word of God. We have planned a series of studies. If you will not read the Bible and co-operate with us we cannot help you. There would be no use in our coming; we would only be wasting our time and yours. If you will not consider what we have to say from the Bible we will have to leave. The Bible is not divided: for the Christian the Old and New Testaments form one book. Both Old and New Testaments were written by Jews, and the Christian Church was composed only of Jews in its beginning.

EICHMANN: (then agreed to read the Old Testament)

CHIEF WARDEN: (to us) He is having difficulty reading

with the glasses he is wearing. (to Eichmann through microphone) Do you want your reading glasses?

EICHMANN: No I can see, the print is large and clear.

CHIEF WARDEN: (to Eichmann) But I will get them for you. (He leaves our side, goes to Eichmann's door, hands the reading glasses to him, and takes back the distance glasses.)

EICHMANN: (reads passage) *For God shall bring every work into judgment, with every secret thing, whether it be good, or whether it be evil.*

HULL: (We point out that everything men have done must come under the judgment of God—*every work into judgment.*) This applies to *all* men. Now please turn to page 269 in the New Testament. This is Hebrews 9:27. *It is appointed unto men once to die, but after this the judgment.* All will be judged—good and bad. I will be judged, you will be judged, all men will be judged.

EICHMANN: (no comment)

HULL: Now please turn to page 552 in the Old Testament. It is Psalm 9:17. *The wicked shall be turned into hell, and all the nations that forget God.* God will certainly punish the wicked in hell.

EICHMANN: I do not believe in hell. There is no hell.

HULL: We are studying what is written in the Bible. The Bible says there is a hell and describes it. Turn to page 278 in the New Testament. Read it—Jude 13.

MRS. HULL: (to Hull) Oh, I cannot tell him that.

HULL: (to Mrs. Hull) Tell it to him, he needs to know.

MRS. HULL: (reading) *Raging waves of the sea, foaming out their own shame; wandering stars, to whom is reserved the blackness of darkness forever.*

HULL: Our time is nearly gone. You have the list with further scriptures to read. It is in English—can you understand it?

EICHMANN: No.

HULL: But you can find the page numbers and the numbers of the chapter and verse, and read.

EICHMANN: Yes, I can.

HULL: Do you promise to read and study the list of scriptures until we come back?

EICHMANN: Yes, I will. (We rose to leave and Eichmann also rose. We again reminded Eichmann to read the Bible verses on the list, and he agreed.)

CHIEF WARDEN: (to us) You do not have to hurry away.

HULL: We will leave now.

CHIEF WARDEN: I will take the Bible from him now and give it back tomorrow after it has been examined.

We said goodbye and told Eichmann that we would be back on Sunday morning. We left by the same way, the only way out, and returned to the warden's office. The chief warden seemed very pleased.

"You have crossed a very great bridge today. I gave Eichmann a New Testament before and he would not accept it. But you have managed to have him *read* in both the Old and New Testaments. This was a great bridge to get over."

"How can such a man say that he is in contact with God?" Mrs. Hull asked indignantly.

"Through your contact with Eichmann, do you think that he is sane?" I asked the warden.

"The chief warden can answer that better," he replied.

The chief warden said: "I am not a psychiatrist, but I would say that Eichmann was sane enough to do what he did and to fill his position. He must have been a very clever man in his lifetime. He must have a brain."

"Yes, that is true. I am not a psychiatrist either, but his eyes seemed to me such a light blue color that I wondered whether that was a sign of a mental condition."

"He is very clever," the warden said.

"Yes, but some mentally deranged people are very clever on certain lines," I suggested.

"I do not think that he has a mental condition," the warden replied.

We prepared to leave and mentioned that we would be

back next Sunday morning. We left, escorted by the prison official to the gate, and drove back to Jerusalem.

This first visit had been nerve-racking and left us tense for some time. It had been a great strain on Mrs. Hull and during the session she found it difficult to collect her thoughts, to find the right German words, to turn the pages, and to read the particular verses in the German Bible. For two days she suffered as though she had been subjected to a severe shock. Yet all this was more a psychological reaction caused by what she knew or had heard about the man, rather than one caused by fear or horror due to his appearance.

As a matter of fact the man did not have the appearance of a hardened criminal. One might say that he looked like a hardened cynic rather than the monster his past deeds would indicate. Eichmann's face seemed more at ease than in the court. There his mouth twitched, he drew it far up to the left side, and his eyes switched from side to side in a nervous manner. There was none of this as we talked with him in his cell. His mouth was normal. Though the pupils of his eyes seemed rather distended, his eyes were direct and his gaze steady. At times a quizzical expression passed over his face and the skin crinkled at the corners of his eyes giving almost a kindly expression to his face. If we had not known who he was and what he had done, we would not for a moment have considered him capable of being such a man, such an inhuman man.

Personally I felt no fear of the man, nor actual distaste. I felt that I had full control of the situation and that Adolf Eichmann was subject to my direction and guidance in the discussion. We felt that from the first we had gained the upper hand by obtaining his agreement to read the Bible. We felt confident that if he would continue to read the Bible, the Spirit of God, through the pages of the Bible, would work a complete change in his heart and would bring success in the task God had sent us to do.

EICHMANN'S FIRST LETTER

Chapter Five ✠

Our first task on our return to Jerusalem was to sit down and reconstruct the events of the day and every word of our conversation. We felt that if these meetings continued, a story might develop from them that would be of both interest and profit to an inquiring world. Adolf Eichmann's deeds had been so awful, the scale of murder so immense, that the world was at a loss to understand how a human being could harden his heart to a degree enabling him to do these deeds. Possibly our conversations would provide the answer.

For months he was questioned by Israeli police officials, and many facts were uncovered and questions answered. But this inquiry was chiefly for the purpose of disclosing facts which would establish legal guilt for crimes he had committed. It was not much concerned with the moral aspect of the crimes; and the questions were not formed so as to bring conviction of moral guilt to Adolf Eichmann. Neither was the questioning designed to get the answer to the question with which the world was most concerned: *How could he do it?*

During our interview I had made fairly complete notes of the conversation. While Mrs. Hull was translating my remarks to German or listening to Eichmann speak in German

I had time to write down at least briefly the gist of the conversation. It was from these notes that we reconstructed our conversation. Mrs. Hull could remember better than I for she had translated every word either from English to German or vice versa.

Following our subsequent interviews, these reconstruction sessions would take from three to six hours and we usually tried to do it immediately after our return to Jerusalem while the matter was still fresh, regardless of how tired we might be. As we drove home to Jerusalem after each meeting Mrs. Hull would usually make short notes on important parts of the conversation or our comments on what took place; sometimes we would stop and write at some length. These notes were incorporated later into the text.

Two days later, on Friday, we telephoned to Mr. Nir, as instructed, to check on arrangements for our next meeting with Adolf Eichmann, to take place on Sunday.

After the usual greetings the following conversation took place:

HULL: Is everything arranged for Sunday?

MR. NIR: No, I am afraid not. Eichmann has changed his mind; he does not want to see you. He is writing you a letter.

HULL: He has changed his mind?

MR. NIR: Yes, I will send you his letter or telephone to you.

This was indeed bad news. What had happened? Had we been too firm with Eichmann by not giving him a chance to do all the talking? Was he not interested in spiritual truths, with death so near? Had the police decided against our visits because of security risks?

It might be any one of a dozen different reasons, but we were determined to see Eichmann once more and to know definitely from him that he did not want us to come. I arranged a meeting in Tel Aviv for next Monday with Mr.

Shitreet, the Minister of Police. We met in his office at 12:30 P.M.

In addition to Mr. Shitreet, Mr. Nir and Mr. Shitreet's secretary, Mr. Rubenstein, were at the meeting. I had met Mr. Shitreet several times before and he greeted us very cordially and served coffee. We talked for some time. Mr. Shitreet informed us that he had been born in Tiberias sixty-five years ago. I then brought up the question of our visits to Eichmann.

"When I first approached the government through Dr. Wardi," I explained to Mr. Shitreet, "I had in mind the need of Israel to protect itself against criticism by providing a spiritual counsellor to Eichmann. I felt it important to Israel from a political standpoint that she should not have a case on her hands like that of Dov Gruner."

Dov Gruner was a member of the Irgun, the terrorist group which committed many of the atrocities during the time prior to the establishing of the State, when the Jews were in active opposition to the Mandatory Government because of its stopping of immigration for refugee Jews fleeing from Europe. He had been badly wounded in an attack on a British police post in Palestine in 1947, and captured. He was sentenced to death by a British military court. While his appeal to the Privy Council, in England, was pending, the Palestine authorities secretly transferred him from Jerusalem to Acre Prison, where he was hung. The Mandatory authorities refused to supply a rabbi or spiritual adviser for him. He did not have the comfort of this ministry. As the facts were made public there was a great outcry by the Jews, especially when it was known that he was denied a rabbi.

I went on to say to Mr. Shitreet that I had only the one visit with Eichmann. At that time I expected to have several meetings with him; otherwise I would have approached him on a different basis. I felt that I must see him at least one more time. If after one more visit he did not want to see me then I would be satisfied.

Mr. Shitreet replied that he was ready to let me see Eichmann again. "I have a letter here from him to you; it is in German."

Mr. Shitreet's secretary, Mr. Rubenstein, took the letter and read some of it to us. He explained that Eichmann did not wholly reject our ministry, but that he felt he was wasting our time.

The letter, as translated, was as follows:

Very respected Pastor Hull and Mrs. Hull:

Our meeting yesterday gave me cause, dear reverend, to tell you the following openly and freely. I am afraid to preoccupy your limited time. My reasons for saying this are objective, as well as purely technical.

a. As for the objective: It was not for political considerations that I departed, in 1937, from the community of the Evangelical religion. My reasons were deeper; namely, I acted upon my conceptual understanding in regard to the validity of ultimate matters. And yesterday I saw again how wide a chasm separates me from the Evangelical interpretations. To mention but one example: there is not only the Old Testament which, in this regard, offers me nothing, but likewise I have no use for the New Testament (with the exception of the Psalms, the Song of Solomon, and the Sermon on the Mount).

In case you should harbor expectations that after a certain number of visits and conversations I will return to the lap of the Evangelical Church, this will never happen. I am sorry that I must spell out what must seem to you discouraging statements, but if I did not I would consider myself a hypocrite.

b. As for technical reasons: Communication difficulties caused by language, as well as the necessity to speak through a microphone, do not contribute to the establishment of the personal contact which is so important in matters concerning our innermost selves.

I will leave it to you, dear reverend, to decide whether you want to continue to see me despite my very naturalistic conceptions and in disregard of the considerations I have mentioned here.

Thank you for your efforts of yesterday. My regards to the kind Mrs. Hull and sincere greetings to both of you.

Yours respectfully,

Signed: Adolf Eichmann

Written from Ramleh Prison,

Thursday, April 12, 1962

This was good news. As long as the door was still open we certainly would continue to visit Adolf Eichmann. We were not discouraged by his rejection of our message. God could work a miracle and it was our duty to do our part.

Mr. Shitreet repeated his remark that we could see Eichmann again. He even went much further and said, "We are ready for you to see him at any time, today if you like. You can see him once more and as many times as you wish. We will arrange it for you."

On the other hand, Mr. Nir, the commissioner of prisons, was not anxious for us to resume our meetings. "It is wasting your time to see him," he said. "He will not read the Bible." I could feel for him in his security problem. Adolf Eichmann had been in his hands now for almost two years. His confinement and protection had been a major problem and responsibility. Nir saw no chance of Eichmann sincerely turning to God and he probably thought it was a waste of both our time and that of the prison officials.

Something of the feelings of these men toward their prisoner was indicated by Mr. Shitreet when he told me that he could not even look at the man, he was so distasteful to him. The wonder is that with such feelings moving those in charge of Eichmann he should have been so well treated. Israel is to be greatly commended for its considerate treatment of its prisoner, this super-Nazi murderer, whose function it was to make the world *Judenrein* (free of Jews).

Mr. Rubenstein did not agree with Mr. Nir that Eichmann

would not read the Bible. He felt that he had read it since our visit. He felt this from remarks in the letter.

A general conversation developed regarding the prisoner. I said, "He is either a great actor or . . ."

"He *is* a great actor," my wife claimed.

Mr. Shitreet said, "I looked at him twice. He has eyes of iron. He is acting a part."

"If he were let loose he would do it all over again," Mrs. Hull affirmed.

"Yes, there is no humility or repentance," Mr. Shitreet agreed.

Mr. Rubenstein suggested, "Eichmann thinks that he has lived seventeen years past the time of his crime, so he has got that much more out of life than his due. He expects to die, but he thinks it was worth it to kill all those people."

"No, he is planning and acting," said my wife. "He does not expect to die."

"He was a very clever man," Mr. Rubenstein claimed.

The Minister of Police said, "When I had to inspect the arrangements for his detention I could not look at him. However, Mr. Hull, if you want to visit him you may."

"Yes, I do."

"When do you want to go?" Mr. Nir asked.

"I am busy Wednesday, but Thursday would be convenient to me. No, that is Pesah; better make it Friday."

Mr. Nir agreed. "We will make all arrangements for Friday, April 20th, at 10 A.M."

THE SECOND VISIT

Chapter Six ✠

As on the first visit we were escorted from the gate by the prison official and taken to the warden's office. The chief warden greeted us with the news that he had given the German Bible to Eichmann who took it and put it in a cupboard. When he saw that Eichmann did not appear interested in the Bible he told him that he did not *have* to keep it if he did not want it. Eichmann said to him, "Leave it here."

Both of us thought this was a good sign.

"I have some more news for you," the chief warden said. "After you left on the first visit the doctor gave Eichmann his daily medical examination. Usually his blood pressure is normal. This time, however, the doctor asked us what we had been doing to him. He said that his blood pressure was way up."

We wondered whether anything we had said or read to him had affected him or stirred some old memories. We thought that we might take some encouragement from this.

I asked the warden whether Eichmann knew that there was little hope that his appeal would succeed, and he told me that Dr. Servatius had warned him of this.

We left then to go up to the death cell. Everything was

as on the first visit, but Eichmann was now wearing a gray flannel shirt and a khaki cardigan.

We adjusted our earphones and I greeted Eichmann with, "*Guten Morgen.*"

EICHMANN: *Guten Morgen.* I wrote you a letter to make myself clear to you so that you would know where I stood. I did not want to appear as a hypocrite in your eyes. (It seemed significant that he wanted to appear proper to us, or was it just his pride?)

HULL: Yes, we received your letter and wish to discuss it with you and ask you some questions.

EICHMANN: *Bitte.*

HULL: We do not consider it a waste of time to try to save your soul. You say you left the Evangelical Church in 1937 for reasons which were deeper than political reasons. You joined the Nazi Party the first of April, 1932. Did you remain in the Church for five years after, until 1937?

EICHMANN: Yes.

HULL: Do you care to tell us what were your reasons for leaving the Evangelical Church?

EICHMANN: When I first joined the Party they asked me to leave the Church, but I did not wish to do so. I remained a church member and did not *at first* see why I could not be a member both of the Party and the Church. (He joined the party in Austria in 1932. During 1933–34 he underwent training as an S.S. guard in the Dachau Concentration Camp. On October 1, 1934 he joined the Security Service of the S.S. He started dealing with the Jewish question in 1935 in the Central Office for Jewish Emigration and later in the *Judenreferat* [Section for Jews] of the Gestapo. He rose to the rank of Lieutenant-Colonel by 1944. The chain of command in his office was: Hitler, Himmler, Heydrich, Mueller [Head of the Gestapo], Eichmann. As a church member he would not be able to conscientiously do the work required of him at Dachau and in the *Judenreferat*.) I was married in the Church in 1935 and the Party was very angry. They became more and more opposed to my church attendance and insisted that I give up my membership in the Church. As to my Christian faith, I was brought up as a child in my father's church and was strong in my belief. Because of this early training and faith the Party at first did not have any effect on my belief. Later I saw that there was a serious conflict between the Party belief and the Church, and I began to give serious consideration to the whole Church setup. As I considered them, I saw that they were all the same—politics, just like the Party. (Apparently at that time he still had a conscience and was looking for something to justify his leaving the Church.) Later I began to interest myself in all religions—Buddhism, etc. Through this I came to the conclusion that all religions were the same, bent on material gain rather than offering spiritual help. *The more I studied the further I got from the Church.* I searched very hard for truth outside of the Church. I did this not because of my Party position but because of my desire for peace in my heart. I started looking at people and criticized them, for I saw that the Church had its Church politics just like my Party, and I wanted spiritual truth. I turned to Hellenistic philosophy. I studied Kant. I read Nietzsche's *The Antichrist.* All this in my search for peace through truth, but I did not find it. *I decided to try and make direct contact with God by myself, and through nature I found God.* In the natural things of life —the trees, mountains, sky, and other things of nature anyone can find God. Man would be stupid to believe there is a God when you look at nature.

CHIEF WARDEN: (correcting Mrs. Hull) No, he said: "A man would be stupid *not* to believe there is a God when you look at nature."

HULL: Yes, the New Testament, the first chapter of Romans, points out that God can be understood by the things He made (nature).

EICHMANN: I take the practical side of the Bible, as I read books on philosophy, and I pick out what gives me peace. I searched for the godly things.

HULL: One cannot take just what suits them from the
Bible; it is all the word of God. If any part of it is of God, it
is all of God. Did you read the scriptures we left for you to
read?

EICHMANN: Yes, I read and studied them all. (continuing) I asked myself many questions before leaving the
Church.

1. Why would Almighty God send His Son to this earth for
man who is no more than a seed compared to the size of the
earth? Man is insignificant and God is Almighty.

2. If God needed to send His Son why did He wait, why was
He not sent millions of years sooner?

3. Then I thought of God the Father, God the Son, God the
Holy Ghost as taught by the Churches. I was not satisfied
with this. I could not find that which would satisfy and show
me the way. Every minister had a different idea and again
I felt that it was all just politics to get people into the
Churches. The world had its politics and the Church had its
politics. I thought of certain churches and ministers. It
seemed to me that none of them had direct contact with God.
They were too human; how could they get directions from
God? I felt that God was Almighty and that He did not need
any assistants (Trinity). That was nothing but the interpretation and idea of the Church to suit its purpose. I carried my
own burden until 1937. Then I found God in my way through
nature when I left the Church. And now for the last twenty-
five years I have had peace in my heart. (Was it peace or
was his conscience seared through giving his whole heart to
the Party [Devil]? Certainly the Devil would no longer disturb him when he was on his side.)

HULL: If you have peace with God—

EICHMANN: *Not peace with God, peace in God. God
leads me.*

MRS. HULL: Then did God lead you here, to Ramleh
Prison?

EICHMANN: (heatedly and very excited) No! No! God

did not lead me here but the— (He was going to say that the Jews brought him there, but out of fear or respect for his guards refrained.) It is not my fault that I am here, and it is not God's fault. The fault was with the Nazi Party. I did not kill anybody. I am not a murderer. I did not steal, I was not a thief. I am not to blame. Even Jesus Christ would not condemn me.

CHIEF WARDEN: (goes into Eichmann's part and hands him a lighted cigarette, with the idea of calming him. He always did this when any tension arose, but he never permitted Eichmann to light the cigarette himself. Eichmann thanked him very politely.)

HULL: We are not here to discuss these things; we are here to get your soul saved.

EICHMANN: Under these conditions (glass separating and speech through microphones) it will take a year to study all this.

MRS. HULL: With God it will not take a year. If you are in earnest and bow your head in prayer before reading the Bible, the power of God will enlighten you.

HULL: Did you know that Jesus died to save sinners?

EICHMANN: No, I do not believe that.

HULL: But you cannot come to God apart from Jesus. He said: *I am the way, the truth, and the life: no man cometh unto the Father, but by me.* I want you to read Romans 3:10 and 23. *There is none righteous, no, not one. . . . For all have sinned, and come short of the glory of God.*

EICHMANN: (reads) I believe that, I believe that.

CHIEF WARDEN: (to us) In five minutes it will be eleven o'clock.

HULL: (to chief warden) We are just through. (to Eichmann) We are leaving another list of scriptures for you to read and study. Will you do so?

EICHMANN: Yes.

HULL: We will come again soon. *Auf Wiedersehen.*

EICHMANN: *Auf Wiedersehen.*

We left and as usual freely conversed with the chief warden on the stairs. I said to him: "I wish that I could tell B.-G. (Ben-Gurion) that Eichmann studied Buddhism and Greek philosophy and point out where it led him in his thinking." The chief warden laughed.

In the warden's office we discussed our impressions of the morning talk. We were all of the opinion that at the first meeting he was acting, but that now he was somewhat disturbed and seriously thinking.

The chief warden remarked that Eichmann's German is not so good. "He is not highly educated, but pretends that he is by his choice of difficult words."

He could have been trying to make it difficult for us. We left then and returned to Jerusalem.

THE NEWS "BREAKS"

Chapter Seven ✠

Tuesday, 24th of April

It happened today. We have kept our visits secret until now. It is a month since I knew that it would be possible for me to visit Eichmann and two weeks since our first visit to him. I had planned that at the end I would make known my visits to him so that Israel would be credited with generosity in providing a spiritual adviser for Eichmann. But the secret did not keep. Mr. Shitreet admitted that someone in the police had revealed the news. He was angry that it had come from his men.

Yediot Aharonot, an afternoon Hebrew paper, was the first to get the news. They ran a couple of inches on the front page. Apparently they only had an intimation of the visits without any actual particulars. No name was mentioned. However, it was enough to start the press on a wild chase.

By the next morning the telephone began to ring and we had little time to ourselves from then on. Mr. Nir had confirmed the fact to them and told them to contact me for details. They did—morning, noon, and night.

Wednesday, 25th of April

Reuters reached me first by telephone from Tel Aviv. I gave them very little information beyond confirming my visits. *Yediot Aharonot* then telephoned for an interview. *The Times* (London) telephoned, then the New York *Times*, Maccabee Dean of *The Jerusalem Post* wanted to know the basis of my approach. I told him John 3:16.

To all I said that I considered Eichmann a human being in spite of his past deeds, and that he has a soul. I said that Jesus Christ died to save his soul as much as mine. I told them that our discussions were entirely on a spiritual basis and that we had not discussed the legal aspects of his case. I further said that I was encouraged by my two visits for he had accepted a German Bible from me and was reading it, and that this is progress with a man who testified that twice he tore up the New Testament in the hands of his wife. I stated that the police officials, Mr. Shitreet, Mr. Nir, and the prison officials had been very kind and helpful. I could not ask for more than they had done.

Later, in the afternoon, the French News Agency and the New York *Herald-Tribune* telephoned. Reuters called again. They said London had asked for more information about my background.

Reuters asked: "Is there anything special about him? At the trial he seemed a very ordinary man."

I replied: "He is a very ordinary, normal man; that is the mystery of him. How could such an ordinary man knowingly perpetrate such atrocities? It is a condemnation on the whole human race that an average human being could do this."

Later I began to consider the man himself and what he had revealed to us so far. The tragic revelation of our contact with Eichmann was that he showed no evidence of hardness of character. I told him in the first interview that either he read the Old Testament as we directed, or else we would not be able to lead his thinking along the lines desired. If he would not read the Old Testament, then we were wasting our time and there would be no point in our coming again. He immediately submitted, without showing either anger or resentment.

The fact is that he is just an ordinary little man who had been set in a job, told what to do, and he did it in spite of the awful suffering and death which followed his actions.

How many potential Eichmanns are there in the world? We might say it was the German character that was able to bring him to the commitment of these acts. My discussions with Eichmann have not indicated that this is so. He has shown no sign of abnormality. His answers to questions and his reaction to my statements have been what one might expect when dealing with any other man on a spiritual basis.

A penetrating analysis of the character of Adolf Eichmann was written by Ilana David in *Israel Youth Horizon*. She wrote: "It is the very commonplace quality so characteristic of the man on trial that spotlights the deeper significance of the Holocaust. The catastrophe of European Jewry has brought home the fearful truth of the totality of man's nature. It is easy and reassuring to theorize about German national character, but there is enough evidence today to show that it requires no specific national character to sink to the depths of human depravity. To be human means to be capable both of the highest good and of the lowest evil."

One could say that in Adolf Eichmann depraved humanity was on trial. The human race has produced a man capable of being transformed by the power of God into a Paul. It has produced a man capable of being transformed by the power of Satan into an Adolf Eichmann.

As Paul wrote (Rom. 6:16): *Know ye not, that to whom ye yield yourselves servants to obey, his servants ye are to whom ye obey; whether of sin unto death, or of obedience unto righteousness?*

It is a frightening and sobering thought to realize that any normal, average man, without being fully aware of the evil of the path he is treading, could be led by Satan to a point where he could even be transformed into an Adolf Eichmann. This is not to excuse Eichmann—there is no excuse for one who yields to Satan—but it is to warn man that *There is a way which seemeth right unto a man but the end thereof are the ways of death.* The depravity of many of the youth of our day, the gangsters, the brutality of a Stalin, all are but indications of the fact that individual young men and older men have yielded themselves to the wiles of Satan, and as Paul says, *His servants ye are to whom ye obey.*

Eichmann permitted himself to become the servant of Satan in the guise of the Nazi Party. As such he must needs obey. His obedience must go on from day to day, from year to year until six million die—*the end thereof are the ways of death.*

Will the world be warned by this horrible revelation of the power of Satan? Will man say, looking upon Eichmann in the dock, on the gallows, on the pages of history: There, but for the Grace of God, go I?

THE THIRD VISIT

Chapter Eight ✠

A schedule of meetings was prepared for another eight visits. We planned to visit each Sunday and Wednesday morning at 10 A.M. Two of the Wednesdays had to be changed to Thursday because of holidays falling on that day, and one Sunday was changed to a Monday. Otherwise the schedule was acceptable to Mr. Nir and we were relieved of the necessity of telephoning to Tel Aviv before each meeting.

Thursday, 26th of April

Our third meeting followed the pattern already established. We had coffee with the chief warden and warden and discussed the fact that the press now knew of our visits. The warden claimed that the press did not get its information from prison officials. He said that it must have come from Tel Aviv. We then went up to Eichmann's cell.

We had prepared our usual list of scriptures and subjects for discussion. The preparation for each meeting was made with considerable prayer and study. We felt the enormity of our task and that God alone could make our words reach his heart. At the same time we wanted to advance step by step in presenting a clear and logical story of the need and possibility of salvation through Jesus Christ.

This time we started a new thing. We wrote out our questions and comments in English and translated them to German. This had two advantages. We could leave this list with Eichmann after the meeting so that he could go over what we had discussed. Again, if we did not complete our study Eichmann would have sufficient information to finish the study himself. From this time on we continued this practice and Eichmann had study papers written out for him in German which together would give him the whole picture of salvation.

Eichmann rose as usual when we arrived. He was always very polite and respectful, except on the rare occasions when he became upset by something we said. If one did not know who and what he was one would say that there was a kindly, patient look on his thin face.

Speaking about him afterwards Mrs. Hull said: "There is something about him that I like but don't want to like."

His eyes crinkle at the corners and his mouth in repose does not have the ugly nervous twitching it had in court and seems to be more human looking. It seems we are softening toward this man. God, no doubt, is making us feel more tender toward him so that we can minister effectively to him.

HULL: *Guten Morgen.*

EICHMANN: *Guten Morgen.*

HULL: Did you study the list of scriptures which we left with you on our last visit?

EICHMANN: No, I did not study them because I was busy thinking a lot about what you have been telling me. You said that all you could give me was what is written in the Bible. Dr. Servatius told me that you were different from most of the clergymen and that he thought I would like to talk with you and know you. I said in my mind, this minister will speak about Christian faith, so I want to make myself clear as to what I believe. I know that there is new thinking in the Christian Church today. The aim of the Church today is to impose the new on the old. Even the Roman Catholic

Church through Pope Pius gave expression to this new thought. (The following was garbled and it was very difficult to interpret or to get his thoughts. Both Mrs. Hull and the chief warden tried to unravel his meaning. Several times the chief warden told Eichmann to talk in a more simplified manner. I have tried to find simple expressions for the gist of his thoughts.) What I believe is as follows: When a person becomes interested in this truth he desires to penetrate further into it. I am searching after truth. This has been of interest to me not only in these days but for many years. I have asked myself: Why do Christians not seek after this truth?

HULL: Seek truth or more modern thought?

EICHMANN: The knowledge of God in nature. Why do Christians not take this into consideration, to look for God in nature?

HULL: What do you mean by nature?

EICHMANN: I will give you an example. The most important thing is the soul, not the body. (Just what we had tried to indicate to him, but from the standpoint of judgment.) My thinking up to this point is based on this modern thought of God in nature in conflict with the teaching of the Bible. It is my belief that I will live on earth as long as my body exists, and after the death of my body my soul lives on forever. What we understand as death is nothing but the setting free of the soul. The soul is alive within the body but not free; it is bound by the body until released by death. The most important thing for man is his soul. What we believe is reflected in our life while living. In the cosmos everything is in order. The creator and leader of the cosmos is God, according to my belief. The soul is born after the body dies (later discussions indicated that he did not mean "birth"; he meant "release" or "to be set free"), and according to my belief of the laws of the cosmos it is blended with all other souls and becomes a small part of the whole. Everything I have said I believe, but anything else which is not supported by the cosmos belief does not interest me. That is what I am trying to say. (His belief very conveniently ignores sin and judgment for sin. Therefore the need for a savior does not arise. One could well understand why such thinking would appeal to his unrepentant heart.)

HULL: It was our intention to discuss today the question of the soul and its birth. It covers something of what you have been talking about. You will find something written on this subject in the Gospel of John, Chapter 3, verses 1 to 7. Please read this; it is on page 108 of the New Testament.

EICHMANN: (he reads) *There was a man of the Pharisees, named Nicodemus, a ruler of the Jews: The same came to Jesus by night, and said unto him, Rabbi, we know that thou art a teacher come from God: for no man can do these miracles that thou doest, except God be with him. Jesus answered and said unto him, Verily, verily, I say unto thee, Except a man be born again, he cannot see the kingdom of God. Nicodemus saith unto him, How can a man be born when he is old? can he enter the second time into his mother's womb, and be born? Jesus answered, Verily, verily, I say unto thee, Except a man be born of water and of the Spirit, he cannot enter into the kingdom of God. That which is born of the flesh is flesh; and that which is born of the Spirit is spirit. Marvel not that I said unto thee, Ye must be born again.*

HULL: This indicates that the soul must be reborn *before* death. After death would be too late.

EICHMANN: When a child is born it is free; it can move its arms, legs, and other members of its body. So a soul can only be free when it is released from the body. That is according to natural laws.

HULL: But a man has a soul from birth. (This was due to my misunderstanding of what he said above.) Read Genesis 2:7, on page 2 in the Old Testament.

EICHMANN: (he reads) *The Lord God formed man of the dust of the ground, and breathed into his nostrils the breath of life; and man became a living soul.* But I do not believe that man was created by God. My belief is that man evolved from a protoplasm. The difference between man, animals, and plants is—man is different because he is the last production of God. (Contrary to his disbelief that man was created by God.) I think that through properties or qualities man possesses from nature the soul is created in man. All my belief is as Prof. Dr. Brierhoff wrote. I studied his book thoroughly. (What atheists and evolutionists have to account for!) I do not believe that man was created by God but by evolution. But my interest is in the spiritual. Dr. Brierhoff could not explain the soul, but I see that the soul is the important thing. Therefore all truth connected with the soul is of interest to me. (There was an ommission of some sentences here which were not noted.) The Church today is a mixture of Hellenism and modern philosophy.

HULL: There is in the Church today that which goes back to its beginning. The Church has made a full circle and come back to first things and first thoughts. We want you to consider what we say and to study the verses we give you. Our time is limited and we have much to say to you. Your way and your thinking have not brought you peace. We want you to put all your thinking to one side and seriously consider what we have to say. Your way has not profited you, but we know that our way can give you peace with God. Will you give consideration to it?

EICHMANN: Yes.

HULL: We have a saying in English: "The proof of the pudding is in the eating."

EICHMANN: (smiles and nods his head)

HULL: *Auf Wiedersehen.*

EICHMANN: *Auf Wiedersehen.*

Our interview lasted until 11:15 A.M. but much time was spent in the effort to understand what Eichmann was trying to say. He seemed mentally tired from his effort to explain his ideas.

The only thing this session seemed to accomplish was that

he had the chance to explain himself, which enabled us to know better how to approach him.

In the warden's office we talked for ten minutes. The chief warden told us that Eichmann's blood pressure was normal after our second visit.

We did not reach him today; we will have to carefully reconsider our approach for our next visit on Sunday.

THE FOURTH VISIT

Chapter Nine ✠

Friday, 27th of April

Today we prepared material for our fourth visit. Eichmann has had opportunity to express himself; now he must listen to us, and our message must bring conviction of truth. We wanted to let him empty himself of his ideas; the best way was for him to explain them to us. Now we want him to put all his thoughts or theories to one side and to slowly fill up with truth. We have great confidence in the power of the Bible to do this work if Eichmann is willing to be convinced. The Bible is the word of God and as such is a "living word." Through it the Spirit of God can bring him to a place of conviction. We will press him to read it fully.

Canadian Broadcasting Corporation asked for a taped interview to be broadcast in Canada tonight. One question asked me was concerning my views on capital punishment. It was not a matter to which in the past I had given great thought.

Jesus said, *Render therefore unto Caesar the things which are Caesar's; and unto God the things that are God's.* I look upon capital punishment as entirely a legal matter, outside the province of the Church. If the laws of the country provide capital punishment for certain crimes and a criminal violates that law, then the law must take its course. I would not want to be a judge clothed with the responsibility of passing such a judgment, but that is his duty.

As we had already pointed out to Eichmann, Jesus said: *Be not afraid of them that kill the body, and after that have no more that they can do. But . . . Fear Him, which after he hath killed hath power to cast into hell . . . Fear Him.* My interest primarily is in the soul of a man, rather than in his body. If a man's soul is prepared and ready, what then is death but an ushering in to a much better life.

I believe that every criminal found guilty and sentenced to death should be informed on the gospel of Jesus Christ and given the opportunity of coming to a place of repentance and salvation through faith in Jesus. After that the law may take its course. The present condition of this world does not indicate a need for lessening present deterrents to crime. If anything, the increasing immorality of this world would indicate the need of increasing the deterrents to evil and crime. As long as man refuses to be led by the Spirit of God in the paths of righteousness, he must suffer the punishment of the wicked.

Sunday, 29th of April. Fourth visit

We arrived early at Ramleh Prison and waited in our car. The guard at the gate, however, did not wait for us to present ourselves, but immediately telephoned to the prison, and the prison official came to escort us in as usual. We had our coffee and went up to the death cell. Eichmann was in his place waiting for us.

HULL: *Guten Morgen.*
EICHMANN: *Guten Morgen.*
MRS. HULL: How are you, are you well?
EICHMANN: Yes, quite well, thank you. (His pupils seem very large, distended, today.)
HULL: Herr Eichmann, I have something very important

to say to you today; please listen carefully. Please answer our questions today with a Yes or No. Twice you have explained your belief to us. You have made yourself very clear and we understand fully what are your ideas and beliefs. *But your belief does not create facts.* Because you say you believe something does not make it to be so. *You may be wrong!* Have you considered that?

EICHMANN: Yes, but I have my belief in God through nature and I believe that I am right.

HULL: You said to us on Thursday, "What I have said I believe. . . . All other things do not interest me." *But you may be wrong!*

EICHMANN: The Bible is not new to me. I read it in my youth and up to 1937. I have read the whole Bible through twice, both the Old and New Testaments, except for Revelation. I have not read Revelation. The Church discussed the Bible with me in 1937 (before he left the Church and while he was seriously considering this step). My ideas of God in nature did not harmonize with the Bible teaching as accepted by the Church.

HULL: I am very anxious for you to read more of your Bible. Please write your name in it; it is your Bible and does not belong to the prison authorities. We brought it to you; it is a present from us to you. *We want to help you,* do you realize that?

EICHMANN: Yes, I understand.

HULL: We can help you. We can bring you a peace that you never dreamed was possible. We can bring you a peace —not a resignation to fate—that will fill you with joy in spite of whatever may happen to you. We can give you in this life that freedom of soul you claim comes only after death. We know of what we are speaking; it is not just a theory with us. We have that peace; it has come through a real experience with God. *Don't you want that peace?*

EICHMANN: Yes, it is the most important thing to have this peace. It depends on where you get this peace from. I studied all that you gave me (list of scriptures). The last one, John 14:6—these words make me think. *I am the way, the truth, and the life: no man cometh unto the Father, but by me.* But how can this be said—Buddhists and others do not say that this is the way. Many other people believe in God.

MRS. HULL: Yes, all people believe in God.

EICHMANN: No, all people don't believe in God. The atheists and agnostics do not believe in God.

MRS. HULL: They are very bold and brave in their unbelief while they are living, but when trouble comes and they are at death's door every one of them calls on God. And you know that too.

EICHMANN: If Jesus was the only way then only a very small part of the world would have peace.

HULL: Yes, that is true, and only a small part of the world has that peace. Not all Christians, even, have this peace. If you had this peace in your heart you would never have left your church.

EICHMANN: I have this peace; I found it in nature.

HULL: You have a resignation to fate; not the peace we are talking about, peace with God.

EICHMANN: It is impossible for me to fit this (Jesus, the only way) in with my faith in nature. I believe that there are many ways to God. The Bible was written by men, not by God.

HULL: God is a Spirit; He uses our hands to do His work on earth. The Bible was written by men but only as they were led by the Spirit of God.

EICHMANN: God has worked through men and through the Church; all are servants of the Lord. Salvation comes through the works of the servants of God. But I cannot believe that Jesus is the only way to God. I have God and I did not have to go through Jesus.

HULL: Faith is a gift of God. You can receive it or reject it. You did not have to accept the Bible we gave you; it was a gift. You could have said, "No, I do not want it." In the same way faith is a gift from God. If you will accept it from

Him you will believe the truth as it is written. You say that you have found God in nature. It is true that one can know there is a God by observing nature—through nature. The Bible says that and I wish you would study about it. It is in Romans, Chapter 1 and verses 16 to 32. I wish that you would specially note verse 20. It reads, *For the invisible things of him from the creation of the world are clearly seen, being understood by the things that are made, even his eternal power and Godhead; so that they are without excuse.* In these verses we read of what happened to people to whom God was revealed by nature, by the things He created, but who did not seek God in *His way.* God's way. We can know that there is a God by nature—the things which He created—but we cannot really know Him as our God or have a personal acquaintance with Him that way. *The only way that we can have a true acquaintance with God is through Jesus Christ.*

EICHMANN: My idea of God is so big that I cannot believe God would trust His Son to be the only way; that we would have to come to God through His Son and that would be the only way.

HULL: God is a Spirit. He prepared Himself a body, and the fullness of the Godhead dwells in that body (Colossians 1:19). That body was His Son. When you get to heaven, if you believe unto salvation, you will still see God in Jesus Christ. Man cannot see God as Spirit, but in Christ God is revealed to man. Jesus said, *My Father dwelleth in me. He that hath seen me hath seen the Father* (John 14:9–10). You say that your God is too great to put Himself in a man, but my God is so great that He can do even this.

EICHMANN: If I would accept that idea in spite of everything, tell me, why did God wait thousands of years, millions of years, from the beginning of creation, and only provide this salvation through His Son two thousand years ago?

HULL: We cannot criticize God. He works according to His plan and in His own time.

EICHMANN: I do not criticize God, but I see Him through nature.

HULL: Nature is a perfect example or picture of the death of Jesus. If I have a seed and lay it here (on the ledge below the glass) it will remain without life as long as I leave it there. But if I plant it in the ground life will come forth from it. It must die—be planted—in order that life can come forth from it. Jesus had to die, be buried, and come forth to a new life. Now, we are buried with Him through faith and rise in Him to new life.

EICHMANN: I do not dispute the fact that Jesus lived in Nazareth as a boy and was crucified and died to start a new religion—to give people peace and help them. I do not argue that this is not so. This is the convenient way to get peace in your heart. To those who can believe this—to them it is the truth. There are many religions and all have different ways apart from Jesus. But who can say that they are not right? When I think of this I find it very hard to accept the idea of Jesus being the way, after believing as I have for twenty-five years. (He felt that he could not throw away the result of his study of philosophy, evolution, and kindred subjects. That would be a waste of twenty-five years' work. This was one idea he expressed. Actually, however, it was clear that he had been so indoctrinated by Nazi error that he was completely blinded to the truth.) Taking into consideration all these other religions, it is difficult for me to believe that only through Jesus can I come to God.

HULL: Faith is a gift of God.

MRS. HULL: Before we are through you will believe.

EICHMANN: My faith is in God, not in Jesus.

HULL: We want to help you. We know of what we are saying. We were hungry for God and found Him through Jesus Christ.

MRS. HULL: We pray for you every day and look forward to these meetings. You must meet your Maker and we want you to be prepared; your time is very short. We are not only speaking about what is written, but we speak from our personal experiences, too. Thirty-five years ago we were not ready to meet the Lord. We thought that we knew everything, as you think now, until God brought us to the point where we knew we needed Him. Then we opened our hearts and let Him make the word a living word to us. This book (the Bible) is written by man, but it was inspired by the Holy Ghost.

HULL: It is like bread to the body, it is life, it is the living word. To know it you must have an open heart and mind and neither argue nor criticize.

EICHMANN: I am not arguing or criticizing.

HULL: According to the scripture, whether you are guilty or not of the crimes charged against you, you are guilty of sin in God's sight, just like every other man. It is because of this that we have come to you. *You need a savior. You are spiritually lost without a savior, whether you believe this to be so or not.* You should again read John, Chapter 3, verses 3 to 6 and 17 to 18.

CHIEF WARDEN: It is time to go now.

HULL: (We prepare to leave.) *Auf Wiedersehen.*

EICHMANN: *Auf Wiedersehen.* (Eichmann stands and bows politely and repeats *Auf Wiedersehen.*)

In the office the chief warden told us that he saw that Eichmann had had as much as he could take so he suggested that we would leave. I told him that I, too, felt that he could not take any more and that he had enough for one day. I told him that it was quite all right; we were ready to leave.

Some of the points we had planned for discussion had not been reached, but Eichmann now had these typed out in German and could study them, together with the relevant scriptures. If he sincerely wishes to know the truth, he will have no further excuse. He can know if he desires to do so.

THE FIFTH VISIT

Chapter Ten �֍

Mrs. Vera Eichmann, the wife of Adolf Eichmann, was flown in secretly, and visited her husband in Ramleh Prison on the evening of Sunday, the twenty-ninth of April. We had visited him that morning, at which time he knew nothing about her coming. They used the same room we used, which of course made impossible any affectionate greeting. It was the first time she had seen him (and was to be the last) since the morning of their wedding anniversary in 1960 in Argentina, when he had been seized by Israeli agents while en route home, carrying a gift of flowers to her.

Twice a visa to Israel had been arranged for Mrs. Eichmann but both times her visit had failed to materialize. Since it had already been publicized that my wife was accompanying me to the death cell at Ramleh Prison, it is possible that for this reason Mrs. Eichmann reconsidered her decision and now decided to visit her husband. Mrs. Hull's visits may have encouraged Mrs. Eichmann in this connection.

For some days before her visit there had been rumors in the press of her imminent arrival, but these all proved false. When she did come, she traveled under a false name, with a companion, and remained in the plane until all the passengers were disembarked and then was taken by security men to Ramleh. Lod Airfield is only a short distance from Ramleh Prison and the press knew nothing about her visit until it was all over and she had already left again by plane.

Following her visit there were many stories in the press, supposedly the results of interviews the newsmen had with Mrs. Eichmann. But no interviews had been given and the news reports were nothing but rumors, most of them false or with the facts different from the way they were reported.

Wednesday, 2nd of May

Over coffee in the warden's office we tried to get a little information of the visit.

"You have been busy here," I said.

"Yes, we have," the chief warden replied.

"So you had company and never told us anything about it," my wife accused him.

"We did not know ourselves," the warden protested.

"You did not know when we were here Sunday morning that she was coming?" I asked.

"No, we did not know; we are not told ahead of time," replied the warden.

I asked the chief warden: "Tell me, what effect did her visit have on Eichmann?"

"I cannot tell you," he replied.

"Well, was his blood pressure up or what?" my wife probed.

"I can't tell you. Please don't ask me. You can ask Eichmann anything you want."

"Eichmann wrote you a letter yesterday," the warden informed us. "It was sent to Tel Aviv and they will send it on to you."

"Thank you. What was it about?"

The chief warden replied: "It was about some of the points raised in your last discussion according to the notes you left him. It was six pages long."

Word was sent that all was ready so we went up to the cell. Eichmann was in a gray flannel shirt and new gray trousers.

HULL: *Guten Morgen.*

EICHMANN: *Guten Morgen.* (He greeted us with a smile and definitely indicated he was glad to see us.)

HULL: You have had a visitor.

EICHMANN: Yes.

MRS. HULL: We were very happy to hear that you were able to see your wife and to be together again. Did you find it hard? She must have found it quite a strain.

EICHMANN: Yes, it was very hard, but she is quite self-possessed and controlled and hides her feelings. She has a very quiet disposition. (Eichmann spoke very highly of his wife. He seemed to think a lot of her. He looked well and happy. It seemed that his wife's visit cheered him up; he was much more friendly to us.)

HULL: Did you know that your wife was coming?

EICHMANN: No, they did not inform me.

HULL: Did she know that we are visiting you?

EICHMANN: Yes, Dr. Servatius told my wife and brothers and family all about you and recommended you very highly to my family. My wife is exactly opposite to what I am. She is one hundred per cent for the Bible; she reads it every day and sings hymns. (Family morning worship.) I never tried to influence her against her religion. (Contrary to his testimony that twice he tore up the New Testament, which he snatched from her hands.)

HULL: Your wife is a Roman Catholic?

EICHMANN: Yes, my wife is a Catholic but we were married in my church, the Evangelical Church.

HULL: Is your father still living?

EICHMANN: No, my father died one week before I was brought here. He was a presbyter in the church, a strong Bible believer. My wife lived for some time near my father's home and was strongly influenced by him in religious matters. I was at war or away from her. His influence was such that she became quite religious. She had a Bible and a hymn-book from my father's church. She did not leave the Roman Catholic Church but she worshipped with my father's family.

HULL: What family do you have?

EICHMANN: I have four sons; three are married. My sons are married to Roman Catholic girls and were married in the Catholic Church. All three married Argentinian girls and their wives do not speak German, only Spanish and English. My youngest son is six and a half years old; he was baptised in the Roman Catholic Church. I urged my wife to put him in a Catholic school in Argentina because they are the best schools there. My wife will live in Argentina. She has been visiting in Germany and Austria for the last seven months. I have many relatives. My three brothers are in Austria. My wife came from Czechoslovakia and became a German citizen when I married her. My three eldest sons are still German citizens, but plan to take out Argentinian citizenship. My youngest son was born in Argentina and is an Argentine citizen. After two months my wife will return to Buenos Aires.

HULL: How does your wife feel about our visiting you?

EICHMANN: She approves of it, and my brother also. Dr. Servatius discussed you with my brother and wife and told them that you were willing to visit me. They approved your coming and have been comforted through knowing that you are visiting me. When Dr. Servatius first questioned me about a spiritual adviser I was very busy in connection with my trial and did not think that there was time then to go into the matter. Then the trial was drawn out for many months and Dr. Servatius mentioned about you to me and said that you would be willing to come. I thought that it would be good to have you come because I have studied so much in line with my ideas and I thought it would be good to get other views. I had thought of asking for a Jesuit priest because the Jesuits, Christian Science, and modern religions were nearer to my ideas of interpretation. Then Dr. Servatius suggested your name and I was willing.

HULL: We heard that you wrote us another letter. We have not received it yet so we will leave a discussion of the points raised to our next meeting.

EICHMANN: The letter I wrote you dealt with four points in the notes you left me. There are other points, however, that I would like to discuss with you. You said that my belief did not create facts, that I might be wrong. I have considered this. I must say that I think my beliefs are more creative. If I accept the Bible as you teach it, it does not fit in with my beliefs. After all my deep studying I would have to give it up in order to believe your way. (He would have to say that Nazi teaching was wrong.) As to the thought that I could be mistaken—everyone can make a mistake. From ancient times people have had beliefs but yet were not certain that they were right.

HULL: That is why God gave us the Bible.

EICHMANN: What I see in nature is the handwriting of God, but the Bible is written by man. You say: *There is a way which seemeth right unto a man, but the end thereof are the ways of death.* This can be true. I do not know for sure that what I believe is perfectly correct. If the wise of the ages cannot understand perfectly how can I be sure. The way you believe is the old way.

HULL: Yes, the old way.

EICHMANN: Forgive me for speaking plainly. If I did not I would be a hypocrite. I ask myself: Why should I follow the understanding of men who lived thousands of years ago when since then there has been great scientific progress and discovery? Have men not progressed from ancient days? Would the wise men not know more today? If the wise do not accept the old way, why should I?

HULL: You will find your answer in the first chapter of 1 Corinthians.

EICHMANN: You say, read Corinthians, but this was written by Paul. I am familiar with the life of Paul; it could have been my life. If I accepted your belief now, I would be a Saul of Tarsus.

HULL: Yes you would; it would be as great a miracle.

EICHMANN: Paul was converted and left the Jewish religion and then went out to convert the world. One question I want to ask: How can you prove that what he wrote is true? Paul was only a man.

HULL: Yes, Paul was only a man. I cannot prove that what he said was true. I cannot prove that what Jesus said was true. I cannot prove mathematically that these things are so. I cannot put it down as one plus one equals two. These things are spiritually known and proved. If you will open your mind and heart to God and let Him talk to you, you will prove to yourself that these things are true. It is not what Paul wrote but what God wrote through Paul. If I did not know that our faith is true, I would not come here. If there was a doubt whether I was right or not, if there was the possibility that I am wrong, I would not waste my time or your time in coming here. I *know* because God has made me to *know,* and He can do the same to you if you will let Him speak to you. Then you can know for sure that what I tell you is truth and that this is the way.

EICHMANN: I want to know. One thing I know perfectly, that is that I do not know, I am not sure. (He is backing up in his position.) What I do know is by nature and all that I know is in this way.

HULL: The answers to all your questions are in the Bible. We wish you would read in Corinthians. We are marking down here (on the list to be left with him) and will leave it for you. First Corinthians, Chapters 1 and 15. This explains why the wise do not know, but you can. First Corinthians, Chapter 1, verses 26 to 29: *Not many wise men after the flesh, not many mighty, not many noble, are called: But God hath chosen the foolish things of the world to confound the wise; and God hath chosen the weak things of the world to confound the things which are mighty; And base things of the world, and things which are despised, hath God chosen,*

*yea, and things which are not, to bring to nought things that
are: That no flesh should glory in his presence.*

MRS. HULL: You said that you had read the Bible through
twice but that you had not read the book of Revelation.
Why did you not read Revelation?

EICHMANN: My Bible did not have the book of Revelation.

CHIEF WARDEN: It is eleven.

HULL: Yes, we are ready to leave. (to Eichmann) *Auf
Wiedersehen.*

EICHMANN: *Auf Wiedersehen.* (He stood politely and
smiled.)

On the stairs going down I remarked to the chief warden
that we have crossed another great bridge today in having
Eichmann admit that he did not know for sure that he is
right. The chief warden agreed.

Thoughts following our fifth visit: Jesus died for just such
a man as Adolf Eichmann. The thief on the cross was saved
while he was dying. His brief moment of faith was sufficient
to save his soul.

Eichmann is keen on our coming and his wife and brothers also desire it. Can Eichmann break the satanic power
which has bound him and used him for such an awful task?
No, he himself is powerless to break the chain which he
voluntarily assumed. In his own strength he cannot break
out of the net in which he is entrapped. Only the power of
God can break the power of Satan, and this power can only
be effective through the name of Jesus Christ. If Eichmann
would call on this name and believe in Him as his Saviour
the evil power would be broken and Eichmann would be
spiritually free. May God give us wisdom to lead Eichmann
to this knowledge of the truth.

On the whole the press of Israel has been very favorable
to our visiting Eichmann and apparently thinks that the government did right in providing a spiritual adviser for him.
Two of the Hebrew papers, however, were critical, one was

from a political and the other from a religious standpoint. One of the editors was a friend of mine and had at times written very favorable articles about us and our help to Israel. However, in the May first issue of his paper he made some remarks which I felt should be answered so that his readers might know the facts. Ninety per cent of his article was very favorable, almost embarrassingly so. But at the end he questioned my motives in visiting Eichmann and suggested that it might be all right for the government to permit my visiting him once to take his confession, but that no further visits should be allowed. I wrote a letter to him in reply and asked that it be given the same prominence that he gave his own article. It was. He put it in the center of the page with a conspicuous margin around it. My letter was as follows:

Jerusalem, Israel,
3rd of May, 1962.

Mr. R——, (Editor,)
Tel Aviv, Israel.
Dear Mr. R.

It was with grievous feelings that I read the words of your article about me in the first of May issue of your paper.

First of all, no one could be quite so "wonderful" and worthy of praise as you claim the Rev. William L. Hull to be. But if he were, could he at the same time be so low as to be doing the task you mention merely for publicity? Would such a "pure" character be capable of stooping so low?

For your information I would tell you that the police agreed to my visiting Eichmann about thirty days before the news broke in *Yediot Aharonot* on the 24th of April and within hours had spanned oceans and continents. I had already begun my visits to Eichmann some thirteen days before the news was out. I certainly must have a very poor publicity agent if it took this long to persuade the press that the matter was newsworthy.

I have friends in the press, not the least of whom is Mr. R——, and some of them upbraided me for not breaking the news to them. The fact is that I told no one in the press or connected with it as I did not want the news published until the matter was completed. Whatever information was given originally concerning the matter must have come from some section of the police.

Secondly, you are opposed to Israel providing spiritual advice to Eichmann and demand that the government stop my visits at once. I believe that you are sincere in thinking that such a move would be for the good of Israel. Yet, if Israel now stops my seeing Adolf Eichmann she will commit a very grave diplomatic error and will condemn herself in the eyes of all Christian nations and people.

It should not be necessary to remind you of the circumstances surrounding the death of Dov Gruner. It was not necessary to remind me of this tragedy, either, when the trial of Adolf Eichmann began. Do not say to me not to mention the two names in the same breath, there is a distinct parallel in one aspect of the two cases. As you know Dov Gruner was hanged without the benefit of a rabbi. In order to keep his hanging secret, no spiritual adviser was permitted to him. The outcry in the Hebrew press and other papers was considerable and justified. The deed added one of the blackest pages to the history of England's administration of the Mandate in Palestine. Would you have the same criticism hurled at Israel by the Christian world after the death of Adolf Eichmann?

If I have done anything at all to help Israel during my twenty-seven years' residence in Jerusalem and my several speaking tours abroad, all of it added together would not equal nor even approach in value what I am now doing for Israel in visiting Eichmann as his spiritual adviser. The publicity given in the Christian world to this generous act upon the part of Israel will have a very favorable reaction and create a sympathetic attitude toward Israel in their handling of the Eichmann case.

It is not my objective to try and save the body of Adolf Eichmann. We have not discussed his trial or deeds with him in any way. Such things are strictly legal matters and though I attended his trial, I have not and do not contemplate making any appeal on his behalf.

We did not approach this matter lightheartedly. During our first visit Mrs. Hull was extremely nervous facing this killer of more than six million Jews and Gentiles and for two days after she was sick and completely enervated due to the shock of this meeting. I do consider it my duty, however, as a Christian minister to offer the hope of salvation through Jesus Christ to every man, for *all have sinned and come short of the glory of God.*

Finally, as to where Adolf Eichmann will go after his death, this is a matter in the hands of God. In the New Testament it is written: *It is appointed unto man once to die, and after this the judgment.* Judgment of the soul is God's prerogative alone. I believe that Adolf Eichmann is a human being and has a soul, a guilty soul. But I also believe that Jesus Christ died for his soul as much as for mine.

Sincerely yours,

(Rev.) William L. Hull

THE SIXTH VISIT

Chapter Eleven ✠

Monday, 7th of May

It had been arranged for David Rubinger to photograph us coming and going at Ramleh Prison. He was commissioned by *Time* and by the Toronto *Star Weekly*. Both papers later used the pictures. This was to be our sixth visit. It was becoming almost a habit with us, but we were by no means satisfied with any progress we had made. We realized, probably better than Eichmann did, that the possibility of his appeal's succeeding was almost nil. We felt that his time was short and that it was now or never with him. More than ever we were making it a matter of prayer, for God alone could break down Satan's power which held him.

There had been a report in the local press that Eichmann had a heart attack. We asked the chief warden about this and he said that there was no truth to it. I rather suspect that it originated through my mentioning to someone that his blood pressure was up after our first visit. It would be child's play for the press to make this into a heart attack.

I also asked the chief warden whether the press could have reached Mrs. Eichmann and gotten information while she was in Israel. The reply was that she was guarded every minute and it was not likely that any newsman could reach her. There was always the possibility, however, that someone might have been able to speak with the lady who accompanied her to Israel.

The letter which Eichmann had written to me after our fourth visit had been checked by security and returned to the warden to deliver to me. It was in German. I looked forward with anticipation to its translation. We started on our way to go up once more to the death cell.

Eichmann greeted us as usual and we sat down, adjusted our earphones, and prepared our Bible and notes for the interview.

HULL: It was reported in the press that you had a letter from a sixteen-year-old Canadian girl. Was this report true?

EICHMANN: *Jawohl.* (He had used this word constantly in the court, but this was the first time he had used it with us.) When I arrived in Israel I received over a thousand letters of all kinds. This one I gave to Dr. Servatius and asked him to reply to it. When my wife visited me I happened to mention it to her and asked her to get it from Dr. Servatius and to answer it.

HULL: It was said that she wrote and asked you to adopt her. Is that true?

EICHMANN: How did this get out—there must be a leakage here. No! Decidedly no! She never wrote anything about wanting to be adopted. She was a student in Canada and sent the letter when I first came to Israel. She wrote in German and said that she wished that I had been her father, but there was no mention in her letter of adoption. (Eichmann was much annoyed that the matter had become public.) I have been busy writing my family and so did not have much time, but there are some points I want to discuss from the last list. (At this point the chief warden brought him a cigarette and ash tray. He must have thought Eichmann was disturbed.) On page two, you have written: "We who look at the fulfilled promise and those who looked ahead to the promised fulfillment are saved by the same sacrifice." (This was in answer to his question on our fourth visit as to why God waited so long to send a Saviour if Jesus Christ was indeed the Saviour.) This is connected with what my brother wrote. My brother Emmanuel is a journalist and he wrote asking me some questions. He has a pessimistic view on life. One of the questions he asked me was: What is the final end of humanity? He asked me: What does the future hold? I am impatient that I cannot deal directly with my brother. I believe as some philosophers taught that every man's future is predestined by the highest power. This is my point of view and I believe that it is not so complicated or involved as the Christian view. This brought me to this point on page two of your memo. I considered your answer, but I am not persuaded by it for it does not agree with my reasoning. Christians believe in the death of Jesus Christ and His resurrection, that this enables them to be saved and to live again. You mention Abraham who lived two thousand years before Christ. I know that the Jews are still waiting for the Messiah and that the Christians believe that Jesus was the Messiah. I understand that this is the difference between Christianity and Judaism. You wrote that though Abraham died two thousand years before Christ he was saved by the yet-future death of Christ. This thought does not change my mind; it is not logical to me and not in accord with my ideas. It seems very complicated and I cannot figure it out.

HULL: (putting pencil upright on window sill between myself and Eichmann) This represents the cross. Abraham (pointing to left side of window) lived here in history. God promised him that the cross would come. (taking down pencil) The cross was not there then but Abraham looked forward in faith to the day when it would be there, and by this faith he was saved. (putting pencil up again) Then came the cross, the crucifixion of Jesus, and we (pointing to right hand side of window) look back to the cross in faith, believing that Jesus died to save us. It is not complicated, it is very simple.

EICHMANN: There are possibly three billion people or more in the world today, Jews, Christians, and others. Possibly one third are saved through believing. The other two thirds do not believe. Are they lost?

HULL: Yes, they are all lost.

EICHMANN: I cannot believe this. The love of God is so great that He would not let two thirds of the people of the world die. My logic does not accept this. This question must be settled before I can go further. God is almighty, all powerful; could He not make people believe?

HULL: If God *made* people believe it would not be faith.

EICHMANN: Such a God is not almighty. An almighty God could make people believe.

HULL: Then God would not have given man a free will. Man would be a controlled being without a will or mind of his own. He would not have the liberty to choose for himself.

EICHMANN: Spinoza writes that there is no evil in man and nothing wicked on earth. Spinoza writes that God is almighty.

HULL: (interrupting) What kind of a friend do you want? Do you want someone who is forced to be your friend? Or do you want a person to be your friend because he *loves* you?

EICHMANN: That is a good illustration, but a doubt remains in my mind. The point is debatable. For millions of years God created and prepared the world. He would have arranged, surely, for the salvation of mankind. I have read and studied only this far on the notes you left me. For many years I have been filled with nature doctrine and now I want an answer. I want to know the truth. I would like to believe as you teach, but it is not reasonable to me.

HULL: You say that your way is a new way.

EICHMANN: No, no, it is an old way. In the old days people worshipped nature, the stars, the moon, etc., but only now is it being publicized in books.

HULL: But the way of Jesus is the new way.

EICHMANN: Heathens for thousands of years prayed to the sun, moon, and stars. Now Einstein, Planck, and others also believe in the evidence of God in nature.

HULL: These also were unbelievers.

EICHMANN: Some time ago you said that when atheists or agnostics died they all called on God with their last breath. I am writing my brother to check on this. (He mentioned several names.) How did they die?

HULL: Your brother asked what is the end of man. We have already pointed this out to you as written in Hebrews, Chapter 9 verse 27: *It is appointed unto men once to die, but after this the judgment.*

EICHMANN: I wrote my brother that one can only know the future by comparing with nature. You say that man must die and after this the judgment, but these are not my thoughts. Almighty God, the Shepherd, has only love. He would not condemn the weak if they do evil and not right. He would not judge the weak on the same basis as the strong. (How very convenient for the weak and the sinner!) In man's life God gives him understanding and leads him step by step. The philosophers say some are wicked, some good, but God leads them all.

HULL: Those who hear the gospel are held accountable by God. Those who do not hear we will have to leave in the hands of God. It is not for us to judge them, but all who do hear have no excuse. There is no excuse for you or for us. We have the Bible, the written word. We can know the way, it is written. We are judged by what is written and we must all come to God through Jesus Christ.

EICHMANN: What about those who come the roundabout way?

HULL: Everyone must come to God through Jesus. There is no other way to be saved.

EICHMANN: I will study this further with you. It is hard to believe this with all the other ideas in my head.

HULL: Yes, we must leave now. Are you well? (Because of the heart attack report.)

EICHMANN: Yes, very well. Thank you very much. (He seemed pleased that we asked.)

MRS. HULL: You say that it is hard to believe with all the

other ideas in your head. You say that God is almighty and loving. Then bow down your head and pray before reading and you will find it easier.

HULL: We are leaving this slip for you to study. It is a story (Prodigal Son) in the New Testament. (Mrs. Hull had sometimes said "No" to some things he said, or "Amen.")

EICHMANN: I do not want "No" or "Amen." This is not enough for me. I must fully understand to believe.

HULL: We must go, *Auf Wiedersehen.*

EICHMANN: *Auf Wiedersehen, auf Wiedersehen.*

Eichmann had been very respectful and tried to make us think that he wanted to believe but that he must be convinced. When we crossed him or checked him he was not angry or resentful. He seemed to feel that we were concerned for his future life and gave the impression that he was learning to trust us. He grasped at each sign of compassion from us.

On the stairs going down I asked the chief warden whether he talked sometimes with Eichmann. He said no, that he only spoke to him to give orders. He said that it was the same with the guards; no one spoke to him.

In the warden's office he asked us how it had been. We told him that it was very good and that Eichmann had been thinking and we let him do most of the talking. Mrs. Hull said to him that we had to thank him (the warden) for being so patient with us.

"It is we who are learning patience from you. There are few that would come so often and regularly as you do," the warden said.

Mrs. Hull replied: "But we could not do it without the help and consideration you give us."

As we left the prison the photographer was still there to get some snaps of us.

Today I felt somewhat frustrated by the glass between us and the added difficulty of the microphones and the difference in language. As the discussion became more earnest, I

wanted to be able to speak directly to him. Eichmann seemed
to be earnest himself, and willing to consider and learn. God
help us.

Tuesday, 8th of May, 6 A.M.

For some time now the strain of our sessions at Ramleh
Prison, the preparations for them, the reconstruction of the
conversations, and the battle for Eichmann's soul has been
affecting our sleep. For more than two weeks the telephone
has rung incessantly and newsmen and others have besieged
me for interviews and news reports. It is a strain just to re-
frain from telling what we know, to not say what ought not
to be said.

The result has been that I wake up between 4:30 A.M. to
5 A.M. every morning and lie thinking on our last meeting
or some aspect of our ministry and effort. Eventually my
thoughts crystallize and I become so full of them that I get
up and get paper and pen and write. At times Mrs. Hull ex-
presses her thoughts to me, for she too is under a heavy
strain.

This morning she had a revulsion of feeling against Eichmann. "He was ambitious and still hopes that he will not be
hung," she exclaimed. "He is like a cornered rat. His cell is
small, he runs around trying to find a hole to escape, but
there is no hole, no place that he can chew his way out. He
still has hope, he is still striving, still trying. How considerate
the police are. He has every comfort and those who are there
for lesser crimes are not so well treated as he is. It is only a
God that forgives all sin and can save even a thief on a cross
that would pardon such a one as Adolf Eichmann. I am only
a minister's wife and must do my duty, but I have no compassion or feeling for him.

"Why should he have our time, our efforts. He is worse
than any other criminal. He is hard, ambitious, quick to anger, like Hitler. I see the human side, the graves, the bodies
rolled in. I see how they crushed the little children with their

heels and threw them as garbage down the drain. People made in God's image attacking God through His people (the Jews). They are anti-God—his God in nature is just an act and he has an audience to listen for the first time."

Sometimes we would talk over the problem: That morning I said, "It can only be a miracle if God reaches his heart. Our time with him is short. Have we overemphasized the possibility of a change in him? Is he a normal man? Are we right in saying so or is he a mental case?"

My wife replied, "He is not a mental case to the extent that he did not know what he was doing. He seems to have had a phobia for killing."

"Yet outwardly he is normal," I interjected, "and there may be millions like him who cannot be detected unless their opportunity would arise to kill. Who knows what is in the mind of man? Yet even if God does not perform this miracle of salvation, even if Eichmann does not grasp at this last chance, our efforts may serve as a warning to the world. We have been in close contact with him. We have offered him the chance of salvation at this last moment, through Jesus Christ. If he still rejects, has no remorse or repentance for his acts, it will be shown that he was a hopeless case, his sentence was justified, and the world will feel that justice was done. Today many say that he should not be hung. Our approach to him offers a final testing of his soul. If he remains adamant then the whole picture of his guilt is proved true and his death the least expiation he could make for his crimes."

My wife added, "Eichmann was ambitious and desirous to make himself indispensable to the Nazi Party. He fawned over higher-ups and was willing to do anything to gain praise. He was a little man with big ambitions and willing to pay the cost required to satisfy his ambitions. Even now he would not admit to himself that he was wrong in his motives, in his desires and wrong in his acts. Eichmann was a man with a purpose and a will to succeed, but both were evil. He was sold out to Satan."

N.B.C. asked for a TV interview and had prepared a list of questions. I prepared my answers and as much as possible kept to them in the interview.

QUESTION: What were your motivations in becoming Adolf Eichmann's spiritual adviser?

ANSWER: In the beginning of the trial I felt that it was in the interest of Israel, a Jewish country trying a non-Jew of Christian background, that he should have spiritual guidance from Christian sources. As the trial progressed I realized that Eichmann is a human being—with a soul—and that Jesus Christ died for his soul as much as for mine.

QUESTION: You attended most of the sessions of the Eichmann trial. Did you agree with the judges that Eichmann was legally guilty?

ANSWER: Based on the evidence produced and on his own testimony—yes. I think that possibly the importance of his position and authority as a specialist in Jewish affairs may have been slightly exaggerated by the prosecution but not to an extent that he was wrongly condemned.

QUESTION: What was your reaction when you heard Eichmann admit during the trial that he had torn up the Bible twice during the Nazi era?

ANSWER: At the time it pleased me. If a man who had done what he did had, during that time, indicated faith in the Bible or appreciation of it I would feel that it was a dark blot on Christianity. By testifying to his disregard for the New Testament he disassociated himself and his deeds from Christianity.

QUESTION: What made you believe there was some hope that you might succeed with Eichmann?

ANSWER: When he testified that his father had been a presbyter in the German Evangelical Church I felt that he probably had a religious training in his youth and that some memories of an early faith could be stirred and a flame rekindled in his heart.

QUESTION: Could you describe one of your meetings with Eichmann? By this I mean, what do you discuss, does he participate or is he passive, what are these sessions really like?

ANSWER: Our discussions are based entirely on spiritual matters concerning his salvation. He is quite free in seeking to justify his own thoughts on religion but always polite and deferential. He definitely is not passive. He is very much interested in what we have to say and is always anxious to explain his position and his religious belief.

QUESTION: Do you feel that you are making progress?

ANSWER: We have had a number of sessions with him, all but the first lasting for about one hour. At the close of each session we have felt that we had made progress in bringing him to a place of repentance, confession, and true faith in Jesus Christ as his Saviour.

QUESTION: At the trial Eichmann said that he felt moral guilt but not legal guilt. Do you find that this statement is reflected in the man now?

ANSWER: I feel that he is approaching a condition where he will definitely realize and confess his guilt.

QUESTION: One last question. Eichmann seems a puzzle to most people. Have you been able to reach any conclusion as to what he is really like—what makes him tick?

ANSWER: To use your expression, what makes Adolf Eichmann tick is the same thing that makes millions of other people tick. Such a man must always be a puzzle to people who do not understand the power of Satan. If a man surrenders himself to Satan he becomes his slave and must obey him. Eichmann, by joining the Nazi Party, rejected God and yielded to Satan. Man is either influenced for good by God or for evil by Satan. Once man chooses there is no limit to the good or evil he may do.

(In the light of later developments some of our answers may have seemed overoptimistic, but that was how the picture looked to us at the time.)

EICHMANN'S SECOND LETTER

Chapter Twelve ✠

A translation was completed of Eichmann's letter to us of the thirtieth of April and we studied it with interest. The letter was in response to German notes we left with him of our fourth session. The text of his reply was as follows:

To the Reverend Mr. Hull,

You have kindly sent me two typewritten pages of excerpts from our conversations.

To prevent any lack of clarity that can come about and actually has come about due to the language difficulty, I am here putting down my comments in regard to your writing:

First (as for your Page 1): "You have told us twice that you believe us."

You did not state with *which* of your statements regarding faith I agreed. If you are citing my twice-expressed accord as an indication that I am in agreement with your Christian faith as a whole, then I must stress that there certainly has been a misunderstanding, because there is a *wide* area in your views which I *cannot* logically accept. [There was a mistake here. I had said in English, "Twice you have explained your belief to us." Either the German translation was not correct or Eichmann misread it.]

And when I told you: "of course the Bible is right," I was referring to a book which I read some years ago entitled, *The Bible is Right*. (I cannot at the moment recall the author.) This is a book which was chiefly concerned with archaeological discoveries in different places and cities mentioned in the Bible. (I first read this book about four years ago, and recently read it a second time with great interest.)

Furthermore, and apart from archaeology, I know that the Bible contains passages of the *greatest* ethical significance, which serve or should serve as guidelines for men like me who do not belong to a religious community. A man ought to work with himself to observe these guidelines and to make them a reality.

However, now comes my "BUT." A great part of the Bible deals with Jewish national history and the relation of Jewry to (its) God. I *respect* this national history and these religious axioms and conceptions in *exactly the same way* as those of other people. I do not say this because I am a prisoner in Israel, but rather because this is something I have inherited through my upbringing. *Under no circumstances,* however, is my inner ego ready to accept the conceptions of others as foundation for *my* understanding of God or for my views regarding the validity of "the ultimate matters." I am not prepared to accept anything that disagrees with my *naturalistic* conceptions. *For me there is only one decisive law of divine origin, namely the cosmic law.* According to *my* conviction, this is the *only* law. I have to submit to it whether I wish to or not, *and I do submit to this cosmic law willingly, unconditionally and believingly.*

It is sad enough that to this day governments have *not* made this true and divine law the basis of their legislation. Instead of making the peaceful coexistence of the cosmos the kernel of interrelations, they dive into the waters where every big fish eats the smaller ones. At the very best they live at the level of the carniverous animals. This is the world from which governments derive their wisdom, and this is why over hundreds and millions of years of development man has developed downwards, to become "Homo sapiens." It is even sadder that such governments have the power to bind their citizens to such orders and laws. (I believe one would not need all the fingers of even one hand to count the governments to whom all this does not apply.)

You see, dear Pastor Hull, this is why I ask: What has Christendom, with all its armor, with all its remedies, done to bring about a change? What have other religious communities done about it? Why did Christendom, when it stood at its peak of spiritual and worldly might, not take advantage of its opportunity to reform the world? (Here I could mention examples of what happened to Giordano Bruno, Galileo, and so many others.)

Two (as for your Page 2): You say, "The only way we can come to God is through Jesus Christ."

To this I must say that I cannot believe in this dogma, as I cannot believe in other dogmas which I have mentioned before. Let me just sketch the outline of my thinking here. Here I must think of so many things from history. "Jesus Christ" was the battle cry of Gustavus Adolphus and his chancellor Oxenstjerna. They were champions of Protestantism, but they meant to gain lands for their nation by this battle cry. Oxenstjerna was a pious Bible reader, but nevertheless gain of lands and riches were his first concern. "Mary, Mother of God," was the battle cry on the Catholic side, but what they really meant was to extend worldly power by the force of arms. The sufferers in both cases *were the men who received the orders.*

Three (as for your Page 3): You say that I said, "The soul is reborn through the death of the body." I could never have said this, because in my opinion the soul is not *re*born, but *born.* According to my conception (the natural law from which I deduce this) the relation of the soul to the live appearance that is man is no different from *the relation of the limbs of the unborn child in its mother's womb to the developing whole body.* The child does not need his limbs until *after* he has entered this world, which is *after* birth. Until then the limbs grow as they are nurtured by nature. Likewise, as the human being leaves his human life, his soul is growing. His body is matter, his soul is spiritual. Both, however, are joint energy. After the end of man's natural life (death) the soul becomes independent and free. This is what I said. This is my conception.

Four: You say, dear Pastor, "Whom shall we believe? Adolf Eichmann or the Bible?"

I have no desire to be active as a missionary. Neither do I want that other people should have faith in my attempts to search for truth in regards to "the ultimate matters." Also, I am *not* the creator of such conceptions, because I only seek the truth in the cosmic laws revealed to me by nature, just as other people seek them in the chapters and verses of the Bible and other holy books. *However*, the cosmic laws cannot be untrue, as it is God himself who has given them.

Five: I could say more about your notes, dear Pastor, but it would lead too far today, and therefore I singled out only a few points that seemed important to me at this time.

Adolf Eichmann

1-5-62

Written from Ramleh Prison,
1st of May, 1962.
Translated—8th of May, 1962.

The letter in Eichmann's handwriting was difficult to decipher. Some of the thoughts were even more difficult. It was a disappointment to us for it not only indicated that he was unaware of how near he was to the end, but it showed him as completely rejecting the only means whereby his soul could be saved. To what lengths of nonsense this modern world has gone to invent theories and ideas in opposition to the truth, and how the Devil has used these theories to beguile and mislead! Even as Paul wrote: *They received not the love of truth, that they might be saved. And for this cause God shall send them strong delusion, that they should believe a lie.* (2 Thess. 2:10–11.)

Eichmann's letter was evidence to us of how far he was from believing. Possibly we had been overoptimistic; possibly he had purposely misled us. If so his letter no longer tried to keep up that deception. There could be only one approach now; the appeal judgment was likely to be given almost any day and we had no doubt as to what would be the decision of the court. It was our duty to tell him unequivocally that he could have little hope from the court judgment and that it was a case of now or never as to his salvation. We prepared our material with that idea in mind.

Thursday, 10th of May

At the prison for our seventh visit the chief warden informed us that Eichmann was rather weak. "The doctor put him on a special diet (tea and lemon) for twenty-four hours."

"That is too bad," I said. "Today we are ready to go after him hard. After reading his letter we have decided that we must approach him on a different basis. Time is too short; we must let him know that he is going to die and that he is not ready to die.

"I will read to you what we are planning to say to him. Let me know if you think that it is too harsh, in view of his physical condition. This is the first page:

"1. Adolf Eichmann, we have now received your letter and studied it. We find that it is mostly a repetition of what you told us in these meetings. There is nothing new in your letter. It means nothing to us except this one thing—that you do not realize the dangerous position you are in now.

2. Adolf Eichmann, you are about to die. These meetings can be stopped at any time. There is no hope for you in your appeal. You are about to meet God *and you are not ready to die*.

3. It is now time to stop talking and thinking about your nature theory which you have in your head. Get rid of it. Stop playing with God and with us. Get down to business with God. You are going to die.

4. God never led you to do what you did when you were in the Nazi Party. If you say that God led you then you never knew God.

5. Are you ready to admit that you made a mistake when you left God and joined the Nazi Party?"

"Don't mention the Nazi Party," the chief warden said. "I think that it would be better if you just say your Party, and not to mention the word 'Nazi'."

"What about the phrase: 'There is no hope for you in your appeal.' I have no definite knowledge concerning this."

"No, I don't think you should say that. It would be as though you were his judge," the chief warden replied.

"I will cross it out."

The chief warden added, "It is all right to warn him that you think the end is near, but do not say it in the way you put it. He himself is thinking of the end. Yesterday he had a toothache in his lower teeth and the doctor offered to pull one or two. Eichmann said no, that his uppers were false and he did not want to lose the lower ones also in case he might need them. He would wait until the appeal was heard and if pardoned he would have them attended to. Otherwise, it did not matter. . . . Are you ready?"

I answered, "Yes, let us go."

This proved to be the most hectic meeting to date. Eichmann definitely looked sick, very pale, and thin, his face drawn. He stood as we entered.

HULL: *Guten Morgen.*

EICHMANN: *Guten Morgen.* (he smiled)

MRS. HULL: Have you been sick?

EICHMANN: Yes, I have a little cold. The weather is changeable.

MRS. HULL: (Reads paper, with changes made on it as suggested by the chief warden. She reads to where the Party is mentioned and his part in it.)

EICHMANN: (His face changes as truth is given him of shortness of time. He stops her at point five.) I want to say something. Who says that I am not ready?

MRS. HULL: My husband.

EICHMANN: If you say, Reverend, that I have not much time then I am not prepared to take up your ideas. I have my own beliefs and I hold to them. Your way does not bring me any comfort.

HULL: Are you comforted by your way? Can you truthfully say that you have peace in your heart?

EICHMANN: Yes, although I freely admit that it is possible for me to make a mistake—many people do. But I do not believe that I have made a mistake or that all my ideas are illusions. On this question it cannot be that scientists, mathematicians, philosophers—such as Kant, Planck, Schopenhauer, and others who have studied this subject from creation can be mistaken. They cannot be deceived. It cannot be an illusion. Why should I believe you when all these write otherwise? Do you mean to say that all these scientists and philosophers who have made it a life study, and I have made it a life study, are lost? I am talking about whether I am ready to meet God. You say that the only way is through Jesus; you get it out of that book which is Jewish thought. I don't believe it. Then two thirds of the world would be lost.

HULL: Yes! Yes! Yes! Two thirds would be lost and are lost. Jesus spoke of His people as only "a little flock." You cannot make a detour around the cross; you must come straight through Jesus.

MRS. HULL: The way is straight and narrow and you must come through the gate, which is Jesus. You cannot go around or you are lost.

EICHMANN: I do not believe that God needed a mediator, His Son Jesus. You say that God did not lead me. (he becomes quite angry) I do not blame myself for anything I did. I am not responsible for what was done and *if you are trying to show me my sins and what I have done then these meetings are not to my liking.* (angrily) I want your ideas, not your wife's. You are the priest. I want to know what the priest has to say.

MRS. HULL: Very well.

HULL: We told you once that you will not be judged for your deeds. Your judgment will be based on your faith and only on your faith. The only basis of God's judgment is whether you believe in Jesus Christ and have faith in Him.

EICHMANN: I cannot believe that all those who do not believe in Jesus are lost.

HULL: Adolf Eichmann, if I said to you: "Here is a door, you are free to leave," and you said in reply: "I do not believe it, I will not leave that way," would I then be to blame if you did not escape? Would God be to blame? Jesus is the door that God has made for you to be free.

EICHMANN: I know that you want to help me, but I cannot believe that the almighty God would not be able to save all humanity and that two thirds must die.

HULL: You and I are each but one man. We must first be

concerned about our own souls. For the time being leave the others to God. Let God handle that problem. You yourself must know God through Jesus Christ.

EICHMANN: I know God through what the philosophers wrote.

HULL: It is not by philosophy. We cannot know God that way.

EICHMANN: But I do know God that way and through nature. God leads me. I never lost touch with God.

HULL: If you were led by God now you would repent for all that you did and would now confess.

EICHMANN: I have nothing to confess, I have not sinned. I am clear with God. I did not do it. I did nothing wrong. I have no regrets.

MRS. HULL: Well, I am not perfect, I make mistakes, everyone makes mistakes. Do you mean to tell us that you are perfect, that you never have done anything wrong?

EICHMANN: I never told you that I never make a mistake. Then I would be God. Everyone makes mistakes.

HULL: But even though you did what you did because you were commanded by the Party it was still sin. God does not justify sin because someone tells us to do it.

EICHMANN: I have no sin. I have no sin. What I did was what I was ordered to do. I was a subordinate.

HULL: But do you have no regrets or sorrow for all the people who have died?

EICHMANN: (hysterically) I have no regrets, no regrets. I did nothing wrong. I did nothing wrong. I am clear with God.

MRS. HULL: Your time is short and you are going to die, you must get right with God. You are not clear with God.

EICHMANN: My brother is a lawyer in Linz. I have just received a letter from him. He wrote me that on the basis of the evidence submitted there is only one verdict possible and that is that I should be set free. Any other judgment would be illegal.

HULL: Unfortunately your brother is not here. He is not your judge.

EICHMANN: My lawyer, Dr. Servatius, is also sure of my innocence.

HULL: We will not discuss this further.

EICHMANN: Good.

HULL: God will not judge your life but will judge you on the basis of your faith in Jesus Christ. Are you reading your Bible?

EICHMANN: Yes, I read the passage you left for me to read, about the Prodigal Son. I want to ask you, why did you pick that? Was it because I left the Church? Or was it my belief, that I must do as the returning son? Or because I am like every other man and must return to God?

HULL: The last.

EICHMANN: I agree then.

HULL: I, too, must come to God as a repentant sinner and accept Jesus as my Saviour. If you will let God talk to you and not be filled with all your nature theories and ideas He will speak to you. Give God a chance to show you. All my arguments will not help; I cannot convince you by argument. It has to be the power of God to bring you to repentance and salvation. We know that God speaks to us. God is real. We do not know this by a head knowledge but in our hearts. He speaks to us and He will speak to you if you will let Him. He might speak in a dream, or in the daytime as you read the Bible. God will suddenly make you to know that this is true, that the Bible is His word. These things we speak are strange for they are not material; they are spiritual. The natural man does not understand. Did you read the passage we gave you in 1 Corinthians where it is written that the wise cannot understand spiritual things?

EICHMANN: Yes, but I do not believe that. I believe in Kant, and others, and I have written my brother of what you said, that all atheists and others called on God when they were dying. If they did then they were hypocrites. I have not had his answer yet. I told you that I am ready; I am not lost.

I am ready to meet God. I told you many times that I never lost touch with God. God leads me and He has always led me. I have nothing further to say except that a large part of what you are saying is not new to me. I am in contact with God; I have never lost contact with God. He has led me continually. But I do not believe as you teach.

HULL: Are you willing to let God make you believe? Will you give God a chance to do this? Will you let God speak to you?

EICHMANN: God does speak to me. He shows me all things in nature.

HULL: But now will you let Him make you to know in your heart?

EICHMANN: That is what I said in the beginning. God shows me, but the only way I can know Him is through nature.

HULL: Are you willing to let Him show you that Jesus Christ is the only way? Supposing that we are right, then you are lost.

EICHMANN: Yes, in principle, but I see nowhere that Jesus Christ is God's Son. It is written in the Bible but the Bible is written by man, not by scientists or mathematicians.

HULL: But mathematicians and scientists believe in Jesus Christ.

EICHMANN: I have written my brother to find out about that but I have no answer yet. I want to see how they died, whether they believed at the last moment, whether they were hypocrites as they died. Then I will see how Schopenhauer and others died.

HULL: Why make these men your God and follow them?

EICHMANN: (angrily) They are not my God. These people found God through logic and make it all so clear that I believe them. I believe in God; if I were godless then you could teach me your way. But I believe in God and cannot believe your way. I will not accept Jesus Christ.

HULL: There are two powers. One a righteous power and

one an evil power. Satan is fighting against God and it is Satan that controls you and is deceiving you.

EICHMANN: I have lived too righteous a life for Satan to control me. I believe in the love of God and still believe that God leads me. I do not believe in a Satan. There is no Satan.

MRS. HULL: (aside) That is why he could do what he did, because he does not believe in Satan or hell.

HULL: There is only one thing I ask you: Let God speak to your heart.

EICHMANN: I am satisfied with what I have; I do not worry. Only logic can lead me. I have believed this way so long that I have no doubt concerning my beliefs. *I cannot let you put doubt in my heart at this late date.*

HULL: I do not ask you to believe me. I only ask you to let God speak to you.

EICHMANN: I have no argument.

HULL: That is all we ask. Are you reading your Bible as we asked you to?

EICHMANN: I read the passages you give me to read.

HULL: Is that all—you do not read other portions?

EICHMANN: No, I will just read what you give me. I told you that I have read the Bible through twice. It is not necessary for me to read it more.

HULL: It is time for us to leave. I am leaving this list for you to read and study.

EICHMANN: Very well, I will read it.

HULL: *Auf Wiedersehen.*

EICHMANN: *Auf Wiedersehen.* (He rises and bows.)

We left with the chief warden and conversed going downstairs.

Mrs. Hull said: "He became very angry."

"He is so guilty that he argues with you," the chief warden replied. "If he did not feel guilty he would not argue so."

THE EIGHTH VISIT

Chapter Thirteen ✠

Friday, 11th of May, 5:30 A.M.

Up to this point we thought that we might win him by showing compassion. One would expect that a man in his position, confined in prison and under sentence of death, would grasp at any straw and appreciate any kind word. Yet, although he seemed to appreciate our visits and friendly approach in a way, we became increasingly convinced that we would accomplish more by commanding or ordering than by asking, pleading, or begging. With him the firm approach must be the only approach; he only understands a command or order. To him anything else would be a sign of weakness on our part and of superiority on his.

In spite of his rejection of the gospel I determined that as long as there was time and opportunity I would not leave Eichmann until he:

1. Repented of his sins.
2. Signed a confession of his past deeds.
3. Believed on the Lord Jesus Christ as his Saviour.

Friday, 11th of May, 8 P.M.

Our contacts with Adolf Eichmann until now show him to have been, in my opinion, a servile worshipper of power and authority. This probably stemmed from his desire to be secure and to be hidden behind those in authority. He felt they protected him. In return for this security he was ready to do anything—good or evil. In contrast with Mrs. Hull's previously expressed opinion, I do not believe that he was overly ambitious. All he wanted was protection for himself and to mingle with the "great."

As a result, when it came time for him to be faced with the evil he had done, he denied all responsibility. He felt grieved and hurt. He had given his best to provide himself protection, a shield, and now his judges rejected his protectors and shield and put the blame directly on him. Eichmann feels himself to be misjudged and unfairly treated.

Saturday, 12th of May, 8 A.M.

So far in our sessions we have not prayed with Eichmann in his cell, feeling that it was better not to embarrass him at first in front of the Jewish police, of whom at least four are always watching and listening. Now, at this stage, we feel that we should pray during each visit. We, of course, prayed each morning before leaving Jerusalem and stopped at least once on the road down to pray before reaching the prison. Now we will add this—prayer in his cell—that by it we may find a way to reach him.

Later

Talking with an informed friend today we learned that judgment will probably be given within two weeks. He thought that afterward the whole cabinet would consider the recommendation to be made to the President in reference to a further plea for clemency. I am glad that we have warned Eichmann of the fact that there is no hope for him. He will be better prepared for the pronouncement of the rejection of his appeal. No one we talk to thinks that there is any hope for him at all and no one has any pity for him. Why should they?

It is no honor to be the spiritual adviser to Adolf Eichmann, but I do consider it an honor to be acceptable to the government of Israel for the task. The world does not seem to realize the extent to which Eichmann is guarded. One clergyman in America wrote me that he was coming to Israel and to please arrange an appointment for him with Eichmann. This was before he knew that I was visiting Eichmann. He thought that it would be just that easy. Another in Israel said to me, "It has been suggested that I also visit Eichmann; would you have any objections?" He seemed quite surprised and annoyed when I told him that I thought that under no circumstances would the government of Israel permit him to see Eichmann. Eight locked gates and iron doors to pass and a hundred or more guards to watch him, probably no man in the world today is so closely guarded. He is considered the ultra in security risks.

Sunday, 13th of May, 10 A.M.

Arriving at Ramleh Prison we were greeted by the chief warden and the warden. Mrs. Hull inquired how Eichmann was, whether he was sick or had a heart attack after our last visit. The chief warden said that he had recovered from his illness, but that we had given him a shock.

On the stairs going up Mrs. Hull asked: "Do you think that we were too hard with him on our last visit and that we were not sufficiently patient?"

"No. You were very patient," the chief warden replied.

Greeted by Eichmann as we entered the cell we saw that his face was very dark and gray, and he definitely looked sick. He did not smile.

HULL: *Guten Morgen.*
EICHMANN: *Guten Morgen.* I am very upset; I am mentally sick this morning. For the last four days I have been subjected to severe physical examinations. I don't want to talk about spiritual things today. Maybe I am sick because

I have been here for two years and I am in a sick mood. I have lots to go over and to think about from what you have already given me.

HULL: This morning we had planned to speak only about your family.

EICHMANN: No, I am too sick, I am in no mood to talk. I have been thinking a lot. (Last session we were quite blunt and plain. This, coupled with the unusual physical examinations he has had, probably made him realize that his end may be near. It has been a shock to him. Dr. Servatius, in his interview last March to the *Jewish Observer,* indicated that Eichmann had no realization at that time of the possibility of death and that when he was no longer occupied with the details of his trial and had time to think it might come as a shock to him. This is it. He probably realizes that he now faces the strong probability of imminent death, as we told him.)

HULL: I want to leave this paper for you so that you might write a short thesis for me of your beliefs. Will you do this?

EICHMANN: Yes, I will.

HULL: Please do not write more than five or six pages.

EICHMANN: Very well.

HULL: *Auf Wiedersehen.*

EICHMANN: *Auf Wiedersehen.*

On the stairs going down the chief warden said: "You have made him start to think. I told you before that you had given him a shock."

"Yes," I replied, "we told him last time that he would soon die. He had no thought that his case was hopeless and that he would die."

In his office the warden expressed surprise. "What happened?" he asked.

"Eichmann said that he was sick and asked us to excuse him today," I answered. "We feel that he is beginning to realize that he is near the end."

My wife added: "He is beginning to think, and he is mentally sick. He is now giving more consideration to what we said to him."

Eichmann did look sick and discouraged. He complained that the examinations had weakened him and made him mentally ill. He made a point of indicating that the examinations were unusually severe. No doubt the prison authorities are preparing him for the end. Possibly they have made an examination to determine his sanity, thus blocking an appeal based upon a mental condition. His action this morning may have been a rebellion against the treatment he received while being examined.

We noticed that the chief warden won't look at him. He bowed his head when we called him in to clarify what Eichmann said. He does not seem to have the same patience he formerly had with Eichmann. No doubt the strain on the prison authorities is considerable. The security arrangements are probably more intense than for anyone else in the world.

Too much has been appearing in the papers here and abroad. Today we have decided to give no more interviews or news reports until after the Appeal Court decision. We have an interview with Reuters at noon tomorrow. This will be the only exception.

Monday, 14th of May, 7 A.M.

My wife said: "I cannot get that man Eichmann out of my mind. There was such an expression of fear on his face. He brought that same expression to the face of millions, even of small children, but now he must experience it himself. I would not be surprised if he went out of his mind. Before, he always had a way of escape, but now he is cornered. He is going to get a taste of what he has given to millions."

"But he could get spiritual comfort out of it," I added, "if he would accept what he himself never provided for any of his victims.

8 A.M.

Mr. Nir's secretary telephoned from Tel Aviv and asked us not to give out any further information to the press. I told her that we had decided this yesterday.

Tuesday, 15th of May, noon

It was announced that the decision on Adolf Eichmann's appeal will be given at Beit Haam on Tuesday, the twenty-ninth of May. That is exactly two weeks away. I wonder whether Eichmann has been told and what effect it will have on our visit tomorrow.

Many have contacted us for press reports and interviews. It is a relief to be able to say that I can say nothing further than what has been said. I tell them there is a "news black-out." This does not stop some of them trying to pry out some information, but we have managed pretty well to say nothing, even to friends.

A Christian lady came in yesterday very much concerned. She was one of the German "Templars" who settled years ago in Palestine. I told her that all I could say was that Eichmann was being given the gospel and that she and her friends should pray for the success of our ministry to him. She said that she and some of her German friends had made an attempt to see Eichmann but had been refused. "You," she said, "are the only one who can see him." I assured her again that Eichmann is reading the Bible and that he has been given the gospel unequivocally.

Wednesday, 16th May, 5:30 A.M.

We are back again to our early morning waking and thinking. I am worried about our meeting today. Have we been indiscreet in some of the information we have given to the press? Did we speak too frankly to Eichmann on our seventh visit? It would be a tragedy if our work should terminate now.

This can be a terrible experience for us if the appeal and clemency are rejected and we remain with Eichmann to the last. It will be very trying to be with him during his last moments in the cell and then on the gallows.

In trying to analyze my feelings in regard to Eichmann I see an inconsistency. With everyone else I believe in his guilt and in the justice of his ultimate punishment. Yet God has given me a definite compassion for his soul, as though he were a brother who had gone wrong. I feel toward him as one might feel in dealing with a drunkard at the altar—repugnance for his condition, compassion and pity for him that circumstances had brought him to that condition. Most Jews would probably not understand such feelings for Eichmann. To them he is something inhuman. His deeds make him to them as an animal or a soulless being, one who is beyond any hope or pity.

If Eichmann is hanged a hangman will perform the deed under orders from the commissioner of prisons. Eichmann has pleaded that he did what he did only under orders. Probably the hangman will not feel guilty of murder. The difference is, of course, that Eichmann has been tried and found guilty, while Eichmann's victims were innocent men, women, and children. Their only crime: *they were Jews.*

THE NINTH VISIT

Chapter Fourteen ✠

Wednesday, 16th of May

We left Jerusalem with the temperature at ninety-seven degrees. It is a beautiful drive through the mountains and so many trees have been planted that the hills no longer have their former bare look. On the Plains of Sharon the grape-vines were bright green and the grain fields nearly ripe for harvest. It is a beautiful land and very much more so today than it was ten years ago.

At the prison the chief warden told us that Eichmann was feeling better. "He was under the impression," he said, "that your visits were connected with the physical examinations we made of him. He thought that they were unduly severe because you were coming. I told him that the examinations were routine and had nothing to do with your visits. We told him, however, that we did not want to make him un-comfortable and would make the test less rigorous. He has answered your questions in five and a half pages. It will be given to security to check and then will be given to you. Mrs. Epstein telephoned to say that it will not be necessary for you to keep the appointment with Mr. Nir unless you want to. Mr. Nir wanted to talk with you about reports in the press, but since you have decided not to give any further interviews this will not be necessary."

I said: "That is fine," I did not ask for an interview; it was Mr. Nir's suggestion.

Mrs. Hull explained: "What appears in the press is not always given by us. There are distortions and false information conveyed, over which we have no control."

The chief warden agreed and added: "When Mrs. Eichmann was here she wanted to see how Eichmann was dressed, his shoes, etc. So I told him to stand on a chair that she might see what he wore. The press said, however, that I had told Mrs. Eichmann to stand on a chair, not Eichmann. . . . Shall we go up now?"

At the door of the cubicle the chief warden pointed out that they had installed an electric fan for us. This was very thoughtful of them for it had been very warm in our part during the previous meeting.

Eichmann, as usual, stood to greet us and then put on his earphones and we exchanged our *Guten Morgens.*

HULL: How are you feeling? Are you better?

EICHMANN: Yes, thank you, much better. (He looks a different man today.) I have answered your questions. You wanted a brief thesis, so I have combined questions one and two and got it all into five and a half pages.

HULL: Thank you. It will be given to us later. Now we want to pray before beginning. You can join us in prayer, as you wish.

EICHMANN: No, I will not join you for I do not pray through a mediator (Jesus or Mary) but directly to God.

HULL: Very well, you may just close your eyes or bow your head. (I prayed audibly, but did not look to see what Eichmann did.) Amen. . . . Have you read the list of scriptures we left with you on our second to the last visit?

EICHMANN: Yes, I wanted to ask you about your reference in 2 Thessalonians, Chapter 2, verse 11. (*And for this cause God shall send them strong delusion, that they should believe a lie.*) I have not thought that out yet. No doubt you had reasons for asking me to read this.

HULL: I have a reason for every scripture I give you.

EICHMANN: (nods) While reading this verse I assumed that your reason for this was because of my nationalistic views. Because of the nationalistic ideas I have. Is this right? (This is something new. Previously all his views were spoken of as naturalistic, worshipping God in nature. Now he is getting closer to practical facts and indicating that his views spring from his association with the Nazi Party.)

HULL: This verse was brought in because I believe you are mistaken in your ideas, and all of us must be warned that if we do not accept the truth Satan will lead us to believe something false.

EICHMANN: Then I am skeptical of these words for they do not agree with my ideas obtained by a thorough investigation and study. Concerning the three subjects you asked me to write on, I did not go into the other scriptures on the list because of the time needed to consider and write the thesis you asked for. I read them over, however, and was specially interested in the one in 2 Thessalonians. About the thesis on the three subjects, what was your objective in this?

HULL: I wanted your explanation so that we can more clearly understand your views and see where we agree and disagree.

EICHMANN: Actually the difference is not very great. (God help us! The difference is the difference between life and death.) There would be little difference if Christians were not so dogmatic in their beliefs.

HULL: The reason Christians are dogmatic is because they have had a real experience with God and have their faith not only in their mind but in their heart.

EICHMANN: But that does not prove anything. Originally they created this idea in their head.

HULL: Again I must tell you that I can prove this only to myself. I cannot prove to you that my faith is true, but God can and will if you will listen to Him.

EICHMANN: I understand.

HULL: I would like to talk about your family now, and your home life. You have not mentioned your mother; is she living?

EICHMANN: No, my mother died in 1916, and my father remarried in 1918. My stepmother died in 1959.

HULL: You were quite young when your mother died. Did you remember her?

EICHMANN: Yes, I was ten years old.

HULL: Did you love your mother?

EICHMANN: Yes, I did.

HULL: What were your feelings toward your stepmother?

EICHMANN: Very friendly. I was too young at first to realize very much. She was a good, religious woman and well respected. I have written my brother that a clergyman is visiting me and that he has brought to my memory my parents and my early home. I wrote to him that you make me think of my father; your eyes are kind and honest like his. And I have written of Mrs. Hull that she is so much like my stepmother; she is so zealous and very conscientious for her beliefs as was my stepmother.

HULL: How did you feel toward your father—did you love him or fear him?

EICHMANN: There were seven boys and one girl in our family. There was no disorder. We were brought up in a strict way and we lived a normal, quiet life.

HULL: Your father's second marriage—did it cause any disturbance in the home?

EICHMANN: No, everything was quiet and orderly in the home. There were five boys and one girl from the first marriage; all were quite young. Anyone would realize that with so many children my father could not manage alone and that it was quite in order for him to marry again. We had a cook and a servant but there must be someone to run the house, so my father married again. He met his second wife at a summer church conference center where Christians met. She was from Neunkirchen and was of the Evangelical Mission. They were married by Pastor Saul.

HULL: Did you love your stepmother?

EICHMANN: Yes, she made no difference in the family. She fitted in wonderfully well. She was buried in the same grave with my mother and my sister, who died. There was no difference, and my brothers still go to the cemetery to honor their graves. One of my brothers was killed at Stalingrad.

HULL: Was there a religious atmosphere in your home? Did your father teach you respect for the Bible?

EICHMANN: Yes, in my home we were taught respect for the Bible and they believed as you do. My stepmother was very zealous for the word of God.

HULL: But I want to know about your father.

EICHMANN: I do not remember very much about my childhood. My father was a good Christian. He was for ten years a presbyter of the church, I remember. Protestants are conspicuous in Austria, as the majority of people are Roman Catholics. So one was known as to what kind of a life he lived. There were about twelve Protestant churches in Linz.

HULL: Was the Bible read in your home?

EICHMANN: Yes. We had a calendar with daily Bible readings on it and every morning before breakfast my stepmother would tear off the page for the day and read the passage to us.

HULL: You told us that during the war your wife lived in the same city as your father.

EICHMANN: Not in the same city, but both in Austria. My wife lived in Oberösterreich, my father in Linz on the border between Niederösterreich and Oberösterreich. From the end of the war until 1952 my wife lived in Altaussee.

HULL: But you said that your father had such a good influence on your wife that she began to read the Bible every day.

EICHMANN: Yes, but it was more hymns from the hymnbook. He liked to sing hymns. I was away from my wife seven years. She was neither a strong Roman Catholic nor a Protestant; she was strong for God. But I was away so much I cannot say much about it.

HULL: But your father did teach her to read the Bible.

EICHMANN: Yes, I was away from her seven years and when she joined me in Argentina I saw that she was reading the Bible. She could only have gotten that from my father and stepmother. Her people were strong Roman Catholics; she could not have learned to read the Bible from them, nor from her children.

HULL: Why do you reject the Bible if your father, mother, and wife thought so much of it?

EICHMANN: To honor the Bible and to believe the Bible are two different things. Until 1935 I lived in a religious atmosphere. Then, when about thirty years of age, I began to make comparison with other books and the ideas of other people. We were married in 1935 in the Protestant Evangelical Church, against the wishes of the Party; they did not like church weddings. We were married in Passau, right on the boundary line between Austria and Germany. I was living in Berlin at the time.

HULL: While living in Berlin was your wife with you?

EICHMANN: Yes, from 1935 to 1938, and then I was sent to Austria and my family joined me there and we lived together. Then I was moved to Prague with my family but we lived there only a short time and then in 1939 we went back to Berlin. My wife did not like living in Berlin and took the children and went back to Prague. (She was from Czechoslovakia.) I remained in Berlin. She did not like Berlin—that is why I did not want to go back there, but as the war had begun I was under orders and had no choice. It was against my will that I went there. I was allowed to go to Prague on weekends—Saturday, Sunday, and part of Monday. Later I could only go once a month. In 1945 I visited my wife and from 1949 to 1952 I was alone in Argentina.

HULL: Let us come back to your remarks about the Bible. How can you say that you honor the Bible if it is a lie?

EICHMANN: I do not say it is a lie; it is one thing to say I do not believe it, and another thing to say it is a lie.

HULL: But it is written in the Bible that it is the word of God. It is written, *Thus saith the Lord*.

EICHMANN: The Koran is also a holy book.

HULL: But it is not written in the Koran that it is the word of God. It is not claimed that the Koran is the word of God.

EICHMANN: The Moslems and the Koran do not claim that Jesus is the Son of God; they call him a prophet.

HULL: Again, I say, it is written in the Bible that it is the word of God; the Koran does not make that claim. If the Bible is not the word of God then it is a lie.

EICHMANN: I can believe what is written in the Bible about the last days. I do not say that the Bible lies. I can accept it and believe, or lay it aside and not believe. (Very convenient: take out the blessings and leave the curses.) I would not say that the Bible lies. I would not want to hurt those who believe in it. Now I remember what I wrote to you before, that the Bible does not lie, for I read this book by an archaeologist entitled, *The Bible is Right*.

CHIEF WARDEN: It is eleven. Are you ready to go?

HULL: (to chief warden) Just a minute. (to Eichmann) You testified in the trial that on two occasions you snatched a New Testament from your wife's hands and tore it up. When was this—what year?

EICHMANN: Oh, that was years ago.

HULL: But when and where?

EICHMANN: That was in Argentina.

HULL: Why did you do this?

EICHMANN: There was always love between myself and my wife. We were very close and not divided, even though separated so much. We were of one mind. There was nothing in my past to cover up and she was a very good wife. Our children were well brought up; they were respectful and obedient. Then, when my wife joined me in Argentina I saw that she was always reading the Bible and her hymnbook.

When we had any discussions she would always answer me
from the Bible and it angered me. (He was under conviction and his conscience bothered him.) I did not want to be
answered from the Bible. I could not take it and my anger
would burst out and I would grab the Bible from her and
tear it up. Then she would carefully pick up the pieces and
gather them together and put them away and take out another Bible. I was amazed at how many Bibles she had in the
house so I gave up trying to destroy them as a bad job. Later
she tried not to irritate me by this and would answer me
without the Bible.

HULL: We must go now. I am leaving this booklet for
you, please read it. (The booklet was in German, published
by the Scripture Gift Mission of London, England. The English title was *Daily Strength*.) *Auf Wiedersehen*.

EICHMANN: *Auf Wiedersehen*. (He rises and bows.)

On the stairs going down the chief warden remarked:
"You have been disturbing Eichmann in the past by making
him think of his guilt and of the way to God. He is not so
sure now; you have quite shaken him in his thinking. When
he is shaken and excited he uses long words to confuse you.
Today he was calm, you did not disturb him so much, so he
used words easy to be understood. He said that he would
not offend his friends who believed the Bible by saying that
it was a lie. Yet he was not so diplomatic when you asked
him to pray with you. At such a time anyone could be polite.
He would not have to pray himself, but he could conform
to your practice."

"Yes, I think that he will think about it," I said, "and will
be sorry he did not bow his head and make a token submis-
sion while we prayed. From now on we will pray before and
at the close of each session."

(Several of the "trusty" prisoners know us now and say
shalom as we pass. We had some apprehensions that our
meetings might be interfered with, but it is evident that both
Eichmann and the prison authorities wish them to be continued.)

When we come down from the cell and talk together with the chief warden and warden we act like conspirators planning together against a mutual victim. There is much rehashing of what we had said and what Eichmann said. When one stops to reflect it is strange that Jews should feel themselves such a part of a Christian minister's attempt to bring an erring Gentile back to the fold. They are actually as much interested in the success of our mission as we are. Their friendliness and help encourages us to continue in spite of Eichmann's rejection of our message.

Friday and Saturday I spent considerable time preparing two confession forms for Eichmann so as to be ready should the opportune moment arrive for us to suggest his signing one of them. One form was fairly comprehensive and specified some of his crimes. The other was brief and would only be used as a final resort. My wife says that I am foolish to waste time on them, that Eichmann will never sign them. I, too, feel that I may be too optimistic in thinking of such a possibility, but at least we will be ready if the opportunity arises. We put both the forms in English and in German.

THE TENTH VISIT

Chapter Fifteen ✠

At Ramleh Prison the chief warden handed me the thesis that Eichmann had written on the fifteenth in response to my questionnaire. It had been passed by security and returned.

I showed the suggested confession forms I had drawn up for Eichmann and both the chief warden and warden thought that it would be wonderful if I could get such a paper signed. They thought that possibly after the judgment was given he might sign one, or maybe Dr. Servatius could persuade him to sign. They thought that it might be better to see Dr. Servatius before giving the paper to Eichmann. I felt that if a suitable opportunity arose it should be given to him as soon as possible. I felt that it would create a better impression on the world if the confession were released before the judgment is given so that it would be known that he did not sign it after he had given up all hope, in case his appeal was rejected.

As we went up to the cell, it looked to us as though there were fewer men on guard than usual. This time, too, the key for the death cell apartment was held inside the cell, whereas it usually was kept by the guard in the stairway who would have to hand it into the cell before those inside could unlock the door.

Eichmann appeared even thinner than before and his eye pupils were very large. We greeted each other as usual.

HULL: We will pray. (We did not look at Eichmann as we prayed and did not know whether he bowed his head or closed his eyes. We wanted him to think that we took it for granted that he would at least show some sign of respect. We prayed audibly.) Amen. . . . Now, I want to clarify three things from our last meeting so that my notes may be correct. Your mother had five boys and one girl?

EICHMANN: Yes.

HULL: And your stepmother one boy and one girl?

EICHMANN: No, two boys.

HULL: So there was only one girl in the entire family?

EICHMANN: Yes.

HULL: Did you go to Argentina in 1949?

EICHMANN: No, in 1950.

HULL: When did you last see your wife in Europe prior to your going to Argentina?

EICHMANN: The end of April or early May 1945.

HULL: Thank you. Adolf Eichmann, listen well. Some day or some night faith is going to come into your heart to believe on the Lord Jesus Christ. When it comes get down on your knees and accept Jesus as your Saviour. He will forgive your sins and fully pardon you.

EICHMANN: (made no comment or sign of dissent)

HULL: Now, I am going to tell you a secret. When you are in need, when you are desperate, call on the name of Jesus. All power in heaven and in earth is in that name.

EICHMANN: (made no comment)

HULL: Did you read the booklet we left? Was there anything in it you wished to discuss?

EICHMANN: Yes, I read it. No, it was all clear.

HULL: I am leaving another booklet today. Was there

anything else you wished to discuss on the list I left on a previous visit?

EICHMANN: No, only the verse in 2 Thessalonians that we talked about already.

HULL: Now I want to have a Bible study on prophecies concerning Jesus. There are four pages. I will give you one now and the others when we leave. (Chief warden takes page in to him and gives him his reading glasses.)

HULL: Have you your Bible?

EICHMANN: No.

CHIEF WARDEN: I will get it. (Brings it to him.)

EICHMANN: (Looks over prepared sheet, beginning with Genesis, Chapter 3, verse 15.) This is what I left twenty-five years ago.

HULL: Maybe you made a mistake in doing so.

EICHMANN: You will find this answered in my letter. I want to ask you, who wrote the book of Genesis?

HULL: Moses.

EICHMANN: Moses was a man; he did not write the Bible.

HULL: How do you know? (with a smile) Were you there?

EICHMANN: No. Were you there? (Eichmann also smiled.)

HULL: No, I was not there but I know that God used men to write the Bible. God can speak through men.

EICHMANN: Yes, I know that God can speak through men.

HULL: He even spoke through a donkey because no one else was there, but God prefers to speak through men who know and love Him.

EICHMANN: Yes, and God can speak through nature, too.

HULL: Have you ever heard a tree speak?

EICHMANN: Yes, I have. On the other hand God has not spoken except through nature for the last three to five thousand years.

HULL: God speaks *now* through my lips to you.

EICHMANN: This I accept, it is clear, I do not argue. But

you speak this way. One priest speaks one way and one another. Everyone has different ideas, but the tree never changes. You will understand what I mean from what I have written.

HULL: Do you ever pray?

EICHMANN: Yes, every day. I have not stopped praying since childhood.

HULL: Do you feel that you receive an answer?

EICHMANN: If I had not an inner feeling I could not have answered the questions you gave me to write upon. If I had not been praying I never could have gone through the last two years. If I just started to pray now I would be a hypocrite. (He is very fearful the world will think him a coward or insincere, but does not seem so concerned that the world will think him an assassin.)

HULL: The world condemns you for the things you did during the war. Did you pray then?

EICHMANN: Yes, no one forbade me to pray.

HULL: But could you pray then when you were doing the terrible things you did and so many died as a result of what you did?

EICHMANN: Yes, I could, because what I did I was commanded to do. I did nothing of myself; only what I was told to do. But I never gave up my belief in God or in prayer. What I was accused of in court I did not do. If it had been true I would have acknowledged it. But I denied it because it was not true. It was not I who did the killing; I can pray. (As he was becoming excited, the chief warden handed him a lighted cigarette.) I did not kill. There were people who did, but I did not have to do this. A lot of people had to kill but not I. In the war the church representatives blessed the war effort and what went on, clergymen of the Evangelical Church, the Roman Catholics, and the rabbis. So why should I be blamed for what I did?

HULL: There can be no excuse if one does wrong.

EICHMANN: I did as I was commanded, but I did not kill anyone.

HULL: You made it possible for people to be killed.

EICHMANN: No, I did not make it possible.

HULL: You had some responsibility. I do not think that you had as much responsibility as was claimed in court but you certainly had some responsibility.

EICHMANN: I had to listen like every soldier. Every soldier must do what he is told. He has no right to question and is forbidden to do anything but obey his orders. If I had been an order-giver, in the higher ranks, then I would also have the power to veto anything which was wrong. But this was not the case with me.

HULL: But you must feel some guilt for what you have done.

EICHMANN: What would you have done if you had been in my place?

HULL: *First* of all, I would not have joined the Nazi Party. *Secondly*, I would not have let them take my faith from me or change my religion. I would not have given up faith in the Bible and in Jesus as the Son of God. In which case I would not have received such orders as you did.

EICHMANN: But you are a priest. . . .

MRS. HULL: He was not always a priest.

EICHMANN: If I could have known in 1932 through Jesus Christ what would happen—if I had seen then what the Party was I would not have joined it. Naturally that is clear today.

HULL: But you knew that it was against Christianity and the Wannsee Conference enlightened you as to its evil plans against the Jews.

EICHMANN: You have to understand the Wannsee Conference to know my position.[1] One answer explains everything. There were eight to ten state secretaries and many

[1] The Wannsee Conference was held in the attractive Berlin suburb of that name on January 20, 1942. Fifteen high officials were called by Reinhard Heydrich, Chief of the S.D., the security service of the S.S. Adolf Eichmann was one of the participants and was appointed to write the report of the meeting. The officials attending were representatives of the various ministries and agencies of the S.S. and the S.D. The Conference was the result of an order given to Goering by Hitler and transmitted by word of mouth to Heydrich, instructing him to clear up the fundamental problems of the final solution of the Jewish problem.

Prior to this Conference the Nazis had tried to get rid of the Jews chiefly

S.S. members, one of them a general, and others. There were four above me in order of command. I arranged the protocol but I was only a minor official. To everything I was told to do I could only say "*Jawohl.*" I was a major, or maybe then only a lieutenant. There was a general and others. I was not allowed to voice my opinion. A small man like me could not stand up and say "This is not right." If I had, either I would have been put in an insane asylum or put up against a wall and shot. In either case it would make no impression on the others.

HULL: But it would have been better for one to die rather than six million.

EICHMANN: That was twenty years ago. When it is too late, one can see his mistakes.

HULL: Do you see that as a mistake?

EICHMANN: I am older now and have more wisdom. There is no longer a dictatorship and a war. It is easy to say now what one should have done.

HULL: But there were people who did take a stand against doing the things you did.

EICHMANN: Who took a stand?

HULL: People like Dr. Heinrich Grueber, Martin Niemoeller, and others.

EICHMANN: They were ministers; how could I act as a minister? Yet ministers also blessed the things that were done. Would that not influence me to carry on? (Some mention was made at this point of Field Marshal Erwin von Witzleben and Colonel Oster, but the details were not noted.)

HULL: If you had been a real born-again Christian you would have had the power to resist.

EICHMANN: I thought of that too—years ago—and I came to this conclusion. In 1932 I was twenty-six years old. People

by emigration or transfer to some other part of Europe. They now realized that this could not be a final solution to this problem. The Conference was called to work out ways and means of eliminating all the eleven million Jews in Europe by extermination.

who read the Bible and believed in Jesus Christ signed the Peace Treaty of Versailles. I was young then and impressionable and was taught that the Versailles Treaty was wrong and imposed a tyranny on Germany. The papers mentioned seven million workers being unemployed. Then the Party came and promised to regulate everything and to give work to all, etc. People from all walks of life joined. Even Protestant ministers from Berlin joined the Party. I was pulled in like the rest. What can you say about preachers who joined the Party?

HULL: *Schrecklich!*

EICHMANN: If I had been so clever at twenty-six to realize the true situation, I would have been wiser than everyone else. I saw these people joining and I followed. It is easy in 1962 to talk about these things and see what should have been done.

HULL: Do you repent of these things you were forced to do?

EICHMANN: Yes, I do.

HULL: Would you sign a paper saying that you are sorry for what you have done?

EICHMANN: No, because if I did this now it would look as though I were a hypocrite. I have not just planned this now in prison. I would not have spoken so freely in court if I had planned later to say that I am sorry. But write it out and I will consider it.

HULL: Yes, I will prepare this paper and give it to you to sign.

EICHMANN: I want to study it and sign it, but I am afraid that people will misunderstand my reason for doing so.

HULL: More people will think well of you for signing such a confession than will think bad of you.

EICHMANN: But the judgment is not given. It will look as though I am doing this to be pardoned.

HULL: The judgment is already written. Nothing you can do will change it.

EICHMANN: Very well, if you will prepare this in German I will sign it.

HULL: That is fine. I will get it ready.

MRS. HULL: Are you feeling well? Is everything all right?

EICHMANN: Yes, I am well. My wife and my brother would like you to write them.

HULL: I would be glad to do so if I had their address.

EICHMANN: It is: Dr. Robert Eichmann . . . (He gave me the address.)

HULL: I will write today. For now—*Auf Wiedersehen.*

EICHMANN: *Auf Wiedersehen.*

"You sat in at a miracle today," I said to the chief warden. "That was a miracle to get his promise."

My wife said: "I will believe anything now. My husband prepared that paper and I never thought he would use it. Now I say anything can happen."

(And anything *could* happen yet.)

Monday, 21st of May

We have had ten sessions with Adolf Eichmann at Ramleh Prison. During this time we have carefully instructed and questioned him. We sought to discover his reaction to the gospel and his former experience in Christianity with a view to obtaining an answer to the question "How could he do it?" Our conclusion to date is that the story of Eichmann was not the tragedy of the Jewish people but rather the tragedy of Christianity. Jews do not need to feel inferior as a race because of the activities of an Eichmann. He was not murdering Jews as such; he was murdering those officially recognized as enemies by the Nazi Party. It would have been the same if the Party had declared their enemy to be Frenchmen, or Arabs, or Hottentots, or Roman Catholics, or all Christians, or anything else. Basically Eichmann's actions against Jews were inspired by Nazi policy rather than by a personal anti-Semitic bias.

It was said that in his latter years at school a Jewish schoolmate was his best friend. The tragedy is that as a child, as a young man, and finally as an adult, having been brought up and having lived in a religious Christian atmosphere, he could find himself capable of such an excess of cruelty and utter lack of compassion.

Was the fault in the home? Was it in his church? Was it in his nation? Or was it the result of a world that has moved so far away from God that its members can lose all godly qualities and place national patriotism and subservience before their duty to God to the extent that their conscience can be completely seared? A world with faith in God and in fellowship with God could never produce an Adolf Eichmann.

The opportunity given to Adolf Eichmann to slaughter, and the subsequent notoriety resulting from his deeds, would seem to set him apart from all men. But Adolf Eichmann is not alone in the world. He is not a singular case. The world that has produced one Adolf Eichmann can produce many more. He is but the prototype. He stands alone in his bullet-proof glass-enclosed dock and hears his judgment of death. He is the victim of the accumulated crimes of mankind. He represents the world—to its shame, the Christian world. He will pay the penalty for the crimes he committed, but let it be known that the rest of the world will not escape the result of its unbelief. God will bring all into judgment.

If the death of Adolf Eichmann would bring the world to its senses then it would be well worth while. Better that one man die than a nation. But his death will not accomplish such a victory for God, for hypocritical "pharisees" will merely look upon him on the gallows and, shrugging their shoulders, will turn away with a proud mouthing, "Thank God I am not like this man, he deserved to go to hell."

THE ELEVENTH VISIT

Chapter Sixteen ✠

Tuesday, 22nd of May

A special appointment was arranged for us at Ramleh Prison to offer a confession form to Eichmann for his consideration. The session was at 3 P.M., the first time we had had an afternoon meeting. Some redecorating work was being done in the front part of the building so we were taken in through a side gate which lead past the living quarters of some of the guards and then in by the back door through which we usually went out on our way to Eichmann's private entrance.

Upstairs Eichmann was waiting for us as usual.

HULL: *Guten Tag.*

EICHMANN: *Guten Tag.*

HULL: You were not expecting to see us at this time.

EICHMANN: No.

HULL: I wrote a letter to your brother and his wife. (Showed him my copy through the glass.)

EICHMANN: Thank you. (He seemed pleased about it.) I want to make myself clear so that there will be no misunderstanding. You gave me a paper of prophecies on Christ. It might be thought that I am anticlerical; I am not. Much of that which was brought up in court against me was not true. Since your visits to me I have told my wife to put our youngest son (Haasi) in a Roman Catholic school when she goes back to Argentina, because they are the best schools in Argentina. I also told her to have the boy christened. If I were anticlerical I would not have done this. Another point: All North and South America and Europe is run by the Church. I am not against Christianity, for I see that the only future for my children to learn and to get on is through the Church.

HULL: Good, we understand. I am giving you this letter; I wish you to read it now. It explains about the paper I am going to give you.

EICHMANN: Very well. (The letter was taken and handed to him by the chief warden. Eichmann carefully read the letter.)

This is the letter handed to him:

Jerusalem, Israel,

21st of May, 1962.

Dear Adolf Eichmann;

The enclosed paper has been drawn up for you to sign. I have prepared this as speedily as possible so that it may be made public before the appeal judgment has been made known.

The appeal judgment has already been written and cannot be affected by your signing this paper. On the other hand for this confession to be made public at this time before the official judgment is made known would greatly increase the confidence of the world public in the sincerity of your motives in signing this paper.

I believe that it would be a brave and courageous act for you to sign this confession as it is written at this time and that you will feel better and sleep better and be ready to meet God.

Very sincerely yours,

Signed: William L. Hull

EICHMANN: (after reading) Yes?

HULL: Now, I am going to give you this paper (the confession) in German. Read it carefully and study it.

EICHMANN: (receives paper and begins to read with deep concentration)

The confession form was as follows:

Desiring to make atonement to God and to man as much as lies within my power I, Adolf Eichmann, do hereby now repent of all my sins and acknowledge my unworthiness of forgiveness by God and man.

I do confess that in obedience to orders and instructions from my superior officers in the National Socialist German Reich (Third Reich) I, SS Obersturmbannfuehrer Adolf Eichmann, head of the Office IV B 4, RSHA, did:

1. Arrange for the transport of Jews and others from various countries of Europe to death camps in Germany and Poland as a result of which millions of Jews and others were put to death.

2. Beyond asking for a transfer, make no real effort to be relieved of my command and duties and did remain in my position as head of the department responsible for the final solution of the Jewish question until the year 1945.

3. Remain a member of the Nazi Party from 1932 until the end of the war in 1945 knowing that an important part of its policy was to persecute and eventually exterminate the Jewish race from the earth. As a voluntary and continuing member of the Nazi Party I bear my share of responsibility for all the acts of the Party.

4. Perform my duties in a manner which gave little chance for the survival of any Jew who came under my jurisdiction.

I do hereby testify to my faith in the Lord Jesus Christ as the Son of God and the Saviour of the world.

I do hereby accept the Lord Jesus Christ as my Saviour and believe that through my faith in Him my sins are forgiven by the grace of God and that I am now ready to stand before God, my

Maker and Judge, justified by the blood of His Son, the Lord Jesus Christ, my Saviour.

Signed ....
Adolf Eichmann

Witness ....

Made at Ramleh Prison
on ....

Eichmann read the first two paragraphs and his face began to darken. He frowned and became wild-looking and then, angrily, as he read point one, he said:

EICHMANN: This is false, this is false. It is not true. I am not guilty. I could not sign this, it is not true.

(He reads point two.) This also is not true.

(He reads point three.) I cannot sign this.

(He reads point four.) I will not sign.

(He reads concerning faith in Jesus Christ.) I have not gotten that far yet; I do not believe that Jesus is the Son of God.

HULL: If you do not yet have faith in Jesus Christ you may remove the lower part if you do not believe as is written. I do not want you to sign something you do not believe. I want you to read this carefully. You claim that you pray. Pray about this. There is no hurry. Think it over and pray about it. I have tried to make it very easy for you. The world and the Christians who are praying for you will not be satisfied with anything less.

EICHMANN: Even in the court they did not accuse me of all this. It is not true. I want to take each point—one . . .

HULL: You admitted to this in court. You said that you were in charge of and organized the transportation.

EICHMANN: No, I did not. It was only under orders.

HULL: That is what I have written here in the second paragraph—"in obedience to orders." (I point out this phrase on the English copy and show him through the glass. Eichmann reads it and his face clears considerably.)

EICHMANN: I must wait until Dr. Servatius comes and I will talk this over with him. I would not sign anything until I see him. You wrote this from a spiritual standpoint, not as a legal court document such as a jurist would write. They would sit in court and have a wonderful time with such a paper. They would say: "It is written, he is guilty."

HULL: But what can they do now that the trial and appeal are over?

EICHMANN: I will illustrate: If I say now that I am sorry they will pounce on that and say, "Where there is sorrow there is guilt." They will not admit to any difference between sorrow and guilt. They make no allowance for regret. There is as much difference between my expressing regret from a spiritual standpoint and admitting guilt in court as between day and night. The jurist understands only the word: *Guilty*. I do not have an ounce of guilt.

HULL: You said that you made a mistake.

EICHMANN: You asked me if I was sorry and I agreed.

HULL: *You said that you made a mistake.*

EICHMANN: I said that, generally speaking, I was sorry that I joined the Party. I said that I had made a mistake. It was a mistake to join the Party. I would sign a paper to that effect now.

HULL: Please look again at the paper. Read there that it points out that you did these things under orders.

EICHMANN: But I cannot take out a portion of it; it would distort it. I will think it over. It is very difficult to discuss these things over a microphone with everyone listening to every word and then they publish it all over. But I will think it over. I must see Dr. Servatius about it. The points one to three are judicial and he will have to advise me.

HULL: We are willing for you to do so. However, I think that it would be better for you to sign before the judgment is officially given.

EICHMANN: I understand. I hope that Dr. Servatius will come in time.

HULL: You said that you would sign a paper.

EICHMANN: I am ready to sign a paper about joining the Party, but you have already put my name on this paper. (He referred to his name typewritten below the signature line as usually typed to identify the signature. Angrily he tore the corner of both copies but did not actually tear off any of the paper.)

HULL: You are very careful. I only put your name there so that you would know where to sign and to identify your signature.

EICHMANN: Some people would publish this as though it were my signature.

HULL: But you have not signed it; it is only typewritten.

EICHMANN: That would be enough for some people. The paper has my fingerprints on it and they would use that as evidence.

HULL: Shall we come tomorrow (our regular day)?

EICHMANN: I cannot discuss this paper until Dr. Servatius comes, but if you wish to discuss the letter I sent you I would be glad for you to come.

HULL: Can you tell me Dr. Servatius' address?

EICHMANN: It is Cologne on the Rhine, but I do not know any more.

HULL: Never mind, I can get it. Please give consideration to the paper. I have tried to make it as easy as possible. Consider it.

EICHMANN: Yes, I will. What I have said was my first reaction. I will think it over.

HULL: Think it over and pray about it.

EICHMANN: Yes, I will.

HULL: *Guten Tag. Auf Wiedersehen.*

EICHMANN: *Auf Wiedersehen.*

Later the chief warden said to us: "I told you that he would not sign without Dr. Servatius seeing it. I do not blame him."

"Eichmann looks as though he realized there is not much hope," my wife said.

"He won't think that way if he goes by what his brother and his wife write him," remarked the chief warden. "His brother writes hopefully and his wife told him that he will soon be released."

"Is that possible?" I asked.

"Yes. Eichmann himself knows better than they do. They write with optimism but he does not agree with them."

(We leave for Jerusalem.)

Wednesday, 23rd of May

Today is the second anniversary of Prime Minister Ben-Gurion's announcement in the Knesset that Adolf Eichmann had been captured and is now a prisoner in Israel.

Thursday, 24th of May, 7 A.M.

Eichmann has expressed sorrow and regret and admitted that he made a mistake, yet he vigorously claims that he has no guilt. What is the answer? Has he sold himself on his innocence and through the years brought himself to a place where he honestly believes in his innocence? He must have had convictions about what he was doing when he did it. He must have felt guilt in 1942 even though now he is convinced that he was innocent.

THE TWELFTH VISIT

Chapter Seventeen ✠

Thursday, 24th of May

We were informed last night that Dr. Servatius had arrived in Israel. With the appeal judgment to be given within a few days I felt that once Dr. Servatius contacted him Eichmann's thoughts would be only on his legal case until the judgment had been given. The commissioner of prisons informed me that Dr. Servatius had arranged to see Eichmann on Friday morning. I felt that from then until after the judgment I should give him a free rein as far as Eichmann was concerned and not have any session with him during that time. Eichmann would have to be brought to Jerusalem a day or two before the judgment and remain possibly for a day after. This period would not be a convenient time for me to see him.

As a result a special session was arranged for Thursday morning at 11 A.M. We had gone to Ramleh Prison yesterday for what was to have been a regularly scheduled meeting. However, due to circumstances, it had not been convenient and we had not gone up to see Eichmann. We had not seen him since we had discussed the confession form with him.

Now, as we came up to the cell, Eichmann was waiting as usual, but his smile seemed rather distant. His body was there but his mind seemed far away.

HULL: *Guten Morgen.*

EICHMANN: *Guten Morgen.*

HULL: We did not come up yesterday; it was not convenient. I have one or two small things I would like to get straight. You mentioned a Field Marshal von Witzleben and a Colonel Oster. What was the connection? Who were they?

EICHMANN: I don't remember the connection. Yes—we were talking about orders given. These were commanders; it was in connection with the date twentieth of July, 1944. There were bombs thrown that day.

HULL: Well, thank you. It really was not very important. Have you given any thought to the paper we showed you on Tuesday?

EICHMANN: I had it such a short time that I could not remember the details.

HULL: Did you think about the matter at all?

EICHMANN: The time was too short. I could not remember it at all.

HULL: I am very concerned that you have not yet expressed faith in Jesus Christ.

EICHMANN: I can understand that but I am not yet ready to accept that faith.

HULL: Can you remember at any time, when you were in the Church, that you had a real experience with Jesus? Did you believe in Him then or were you just born into a Christian family?

EICHMANN: From childhood on I never heard anything else but teaching about Jesus. Then there comes a time when a man of the educated class—not everyone, but those who are educated—begins to read books on the science of man, to study philosophy and books on nature, and to begin to think for himself. This had nothing to do with the Party as far as I was concerned. I started to think this way before I joined the Party.

HULL: I want to tell you my story. I, too, was brought up in a Christian home. I went to church every Sunday with my father and to Sunday School. It was what I had been born into and I knew no other way. Yet Sunday morning church services were very dry and uninteresting to me. The "long" prayer seemed endless and I struggled to keep my eyes open during the wearisome sermon. I envied the boldness of my father beside me. Callously he went to sleep. Nothing sounded sweeter to me than the "Let us pray" at the end of the sermon which permitted us to lean forward on the back of the pew in front of us, yawn, close our eyes, and otherwise relax. In spite of this, however, at the age of thirteen I joined the church. Henceforth I was permitted to stay and partake of the communion table as a full member.

But I found no satisfaction in this way and finally in my late teens I just stopped going to church. I began to drift away from things religious. I scoffed at my wife because she had been baptized by immersion and continued to maintain this to be the right way. I insisted that it had no religious meaning.

For a while our lives were not overly worldly, but gradually we went deeper into unbelief and sin. I had read much of the Bible and studied it in Sunday School but really knew very little of its spiritual message. Oh, I knew that the lions had not eaten Daniel, that Noah and his family had been spared in the flood, that David had slain Goliath, that Moses had led Israel out of Egypt, and that Jesus had died on the cross. But the basic fundamentals of Christianity had never been taught me, or if they had, my mind (and heart) had not embraced them.

Eventually I began to say there was no Hell, that God would not punish sinners or those who had never heard. I became quite certain of my position in this respect and quite bold in my unbelief. It led me into paths that I now wish I had never trod. Unbelief will always take a person *away* from God. Fortunately I did not become entangled by philosophical and evolutionary literature as you did. My aim was a good time rather than a serious study of error.

God was not through with me, however. It was strange how He first began to deal with me. Anything serious in the way of religion would have been repugnant to me. I was very fond of playing badminton. We had a club which played in the Anglican church house through the week. God used this as a first step to bring me back to Him. He made me feel that as I was using the facilities of the church to play badminton the least I could do to show my appreciation was to attend the Sunday morning services. I began to do so. Once again I was back at church, but only in a very superficial way. I was still far from God. But God was putting a hunger in me that I had never experienced before. I began to *want* to go to church. Later the Bible took on a new meaning to me. (I proceeded to give my testimony of how after more than ten years of living away from God He brought me back into fellowship with Him and how He changed my life in a way I had not known was possible.)

If you will read the Bible and do as I did God will speak to you and give you faith to believe, for faith is the gift of God. And He will change your life as He changed mine.

(It took about ten minutes to tell the story. During all this time Eichmann gazed fixedly at me and I at him. Mrs. Hull was translating from English to German but neither of us looked at her. I was moved by my own testimony and Mrs. Hull also, but Eichmann gave no indication of his true feelings.)

EICHMANN: I cannot answer on that. I will have to think about it.

HULL: I don't want you to answer on it. But I have something else I want to say to you. I feel that deep down in your heart you do believe in Jesus Christ. You won't acknowledge it, but I believe God has spoken to you and you will have to humble yourself too, and listen. There is a lot of pride in you which you have to get rid of and come God's way, not your way. Have you nothing to say?

EICHMANN: No, not now.

HULL: We will pray now. (We bowed our heads and prayed. Mrs. Hull translated into German. Eichmann did not join us, and I looked up and saw that he did not close his eyes.) Amen. . . . Dr. Servatius is here.

EICHMANN: Has he arrived? (He did not show great interest.)

HULL: Yes, he is coming to see you tomorrow.

EICHMANN: Will you please give him the confession paper you asked me to sign and let him see what you wrote my wife? I would also like you to let him see the letters I wrote you.

HULL: Yes, I will.

MRS. HULL: The reason we have not yet mentioned the last letter you wrote us is because we have not yet fully translated it. My German is not as fluent as yours and my husband will deal with it only when he has the full translation.

EICHMANN: (nods head and says nothing)

HULL: We will leave now; Dr. Servatius will see you. *Auf Wiedersehen.*

EICHMANN: *Auf Wiedersehen.*

Today Eichmann seemed cold and distant. We thought at first that we had reached him through my testimony, but thinking it over we realized there was little response from him. All the time I was testifying he just stared at me without any emotion. The Devil has been busy again.

Thursday, 24th of May, 8 P.M.

Dr. Servatius telephoned and I went to visit him at the King's Hotel. His greeting was very friendly and I explained to him what had transpired since he had arranged for my visits with Eichmann. I showed him the confession form which Eichmann had seen. He did not think that Eichmann would sign it. I said that I thought he might if he (Dr. Servatius) was in favor of his signing it. I asked him whether he was in favor of Eichmann signing and he said that he was.

Dr. Servatius did not seem to have any hope for Eichmann.

He felt that most of the world wanted to finish the matter and that the quickest way possible was to hang Eichmann. I asked if he felt compassion for Eichmann. Dr. Servatius said that he had never been able to reach his heart because of the glass between them, and the witnesses present.

I gave him the confession form to discuss with Eichmann when he would see him tomorrow. He promised to call me and tell me the result. I also showed him the letter I had written to Eichmann's brother and wife.

Friday, 25th of May, 7 A.M.

No sleep today since 5:30 A.M. We are both very tensed by the present strain. What a thankless job this is. Eichmann does not want what we have to offer. He claims to be guiltless, completely absolved from blame because what he did was under orders from those over him. He claims that he prays daily, that he prayed every day during the period when Jews were being killed by the millions, that through it all and up to now he is in touch with God. A man about to die—yet he maintains that he needs no salvation, no pardon, he is without sin!

It is interesting to read of the reaction of other Nazi criminals while they were awaiting trial and judgment by the International Military Tribunal at Nuremberg.

Dr. G. M. Gilbert, as prison psychologist at the Nuremberg trials, had daily access to each prisoner. In his book *Nuremberg Diary*, under the date November 7, 1945, two weeks before the trial, Gilbert reports Dr. Hans Frank, former Governor-General of Poland, as saying:

"'Yes, many things have become clear to me in the loneliness of this cell. The trial is neither here nor there, but what a spectacle of the irony of fate and heavenly justice! You know, there is a divine punishment which is far more devastating in its irony than any punishment man has yet devised! Hitler represented the spirit of evil on earth and recognized no power greater than his own. God watched this band of heathens puffed up with their puny power and then simply brushed them aside in scorn and amusement.' Frank brushed them aside with his gloved hand. 'I tell you, the scornful laughter of God is more terrible than any vengeful lust of man! When I see Goering, stripped of his uniform and decorations, meekly taking his 10-minute walk under the curious, amused eyes of the American guards, I think of how he reveled in his glory as president of the Reichstag. It is grotesque! Here are the would-be rulers of Germany—each in a cell like this, with four walls and a toilet, awaiting trial as ordinary criminals. Is that not proof of God's amusement with men's sacreligious quest for power?' His smile gradually froze and his eyes narrowed to slits. 'But are these people thankful for these last few weeks in which to atone for their sins of egotism and indifference, and to recognize that they have been in league with the *devil incarnate?* Do they get on their knees and pray to God for forgiveness?—No, they worry about their own little necks and cast about for all kinds of little excuses to absolve themselves of blame! Can't they see that this is a horrible tragedy in the history of mankind, and that we are the symbols of an evil that God is brushing aside?' "[1]

The following is a report made by an American padre, H. F. Gerecke, who was appointed to the spiritual care of the German war criminals:

"In August 1943 I went on active service. After having passed through an instruction course I was stationed in a large hospital. From 1944, for fourteen months, I ministered to the sick and wounded. In 1945 we crossed the Channel to France and arrived in Germany on July 15th. A few months later I was appointed chaplain to the high Nazi criminals during their trial at Nuremberg.

"Before visiting these Nazi leaders in their cells I asked myself the question: Must I greet these men who brought such unspeakable suffering to the world and were the cause

[1] G. M. Gilbert, *Nuremberg Diary* (New York: New American Library, 1961), pp. 24–25.

of the sacrifice of so many millions of lives? My two sons were also victims of their misdeeds. How should I comport myself before such men so that they would be willing to receive God's word?

"First I went into Goering's cell. The former Air Marshal took a military attitude, clicked his heels and gave me his hand. Then I made a short visit to all of them. This was on November 20th, just before the trial took place. I passed that night in prayer, asking God to give me a message for them. From this moment God gave me grace, after the example of Jesus, to hate sin but to love the sinner. These men must hear something of the Saviour Who suffered and died on the cross for them.

"There were twenty-one prisoners. Six of them chose the Roman Catholic Church for their spiritual aid; fifteen desired Protestant ministry. Four out of the six were Roman Catholics; seven of the fifteen were members of the Lutheran Church. Streicher, Jodl, Hess and Rosenberg never attended a service. A double cell of the prison was made into a small chapel where we could hold our services. A former lieutenant-colonel of the S.S. was our organist for both the Roman Catholic and Protestant communities. Towards the end of my service in Nuremberg this organist trusted in Christ, and took part in the communion service. The simple gospel of the Cross had changed his heart.

"Frank, Seyss-Inquart, Kaltenbrunner and von Papen attended the Roman Catholic services. Keitel, von Ribbentrop, Raeder, Dönitz, von Neurath, Speer, Schacht, Frick, Funk, Fritsche, von Schirach, Sauckel and Goering formed my congregation. We used to sing three hymns, read portions of the scripture, and then give a short address, closing with prayer. There was never any trouble or difficulty.

"Keitel, von Ribbentrop, Sauckel, Raeder, Speer, Fritsche and von Schirach took part in the communion service. Sauckel was the first who opened his heart to the gospel. He was the father of ten children and had a Christian wife. After a few visits we knelt down by his bed, and he prayed the publican's prayer, 'Lord be merciful to me a sinner.' I know that he was perfectly sincere.

"Then Fritsche, von Schirach and Speer asked permission to take the communion. As I saw these three men receiving the bread and wine I was seized with emotion, for God had worked mightily through His word and Spirit in their hearts, and as repentant sinners they accepted pardon through Christ. Raeder, the chief of the German Navy, zealously read his Bible. He often came to me with difficult passages, and he took the communion with us.

"Keitel, the chief of the German Army staff, asked me to convey his thanks to those who had provided for their spiritual welfare, being criminals. With tears he said, 'They have helped me more than they could have imagined, may Christ sustain me.'

"With von Ribbentrop at first I found no response, but later on he also commenced to read the Bible. Then followed the promulgation of the sentences. Goering, von Ribbentrop, Keitel, Kaltenbrunner, Rosenberg, Frank, Frick, Streicher, Sauckel, Jodl and Seyss-Inquart were condemned to death by hanging; Hess, Funk and Raeder to prison for life; von Schirach and Speer to twenty years; von Neurath to fifteen and Dönitz to ten years. Schacht, von Papen and Fritsche were acquitted.

"The greater part of the remaining time I spent in the condemned cells. Through a favor of the prosecution, the condemned men were allowed to see their wives once more. It was a very sad meeting. I heard von Ribbentrop ask his wife to promise to bring up their children in the fear of the Lord. Sauckel asked his wife to vow to bring up their numerous family beneath the cross of Jesus. Goering asked what his little daughter, Edda, had said when she heard his sentence, and had to hear that the child hoped to meet her Daddy in heaven. This affected him, it was the first time I had seen him in tears.

"Day and night I remained with those who had committed their souls to God. I visited some of them five times daily.

Von Ribbentrop read his Bible the greater part of the day. Keitel was most moved by the portions which spoke of the redeeming power of the blood of Christ. Sauckel was very upset and said many times that he would collapse before the execution of the sentence. He prayed out loud continually, 'O God be merciful to me a sinner.' These three took communion for the last time with me in their cells. God had changed their hearts, and now in the presence of death and having lost all material things and their unworthy lives they were able to rely on the promises of God for lost sinners.

"On the evening before the execution of the sentences I had a long interview with Goering. I put before him the necessity of preparing himself to meet God. In the course of our conversation he ridiculed certain Bible truths, and refused to accept that Christ died for sinners. It was a conscious denial of the power of the blood. 'Death is death' was the substance of his last words. As I recalled to him the hope of his little daughter to meet him in heaven, he replied, 'She believes in her manner and I in mine.' An hour later I heard many agitated voices and then I learned that Goering had taken his life. His heart was still beating when I entered his cell, but when I questioned him there was no answer. A small empty glass tube lay on his breast. He had gone into eternity —a frightful end!

"The hour of the execution of the sentences approached. Now that Goering was dead von Ribbentrop was the first to mount the gallows. Before he left his cell he declared that he put all his confidence in the blood of the Lamb that took away the guilt of the world. He prayed that God would have mercy on his soul. Then came the order to proceed to the execution chamber. His hands were bound. He mounted the thirteen steps to the gallows. I uttered a last prayer and he was no more. Keitel also went into eternity confiding in the pardoning grace of God. Then Sauckel went to his death. With a last greeting to his wife and children and a last prayer he exchanged his earthly life for an eternal one.

"Frick assured me before his death that he believed also in the cleansing blood; and that during our simple gospel services he had personally met Jesus Christ.

"Of the last group first was Rosenberg, who had constantly refused all spiritual aid. To my request if I might pray for him, he replied with a smile, 'No thank you.' He lived and died without a Saviour. Now came Streicher's end. At first he refused to give his name, but as the moment of the execution came he mentioned the name of his wife and went into eternity with a cry of, 'Heil Hitler.' A dreadful end.

"The sincere repentance that God worked in the lives of those who, according to human estimation, were only worthy of the deepest infamy, may give perhaps a ray of hope to those who have corrupted their lives through sin. *The blood of Jesus Christ his Son cleanseth us from all sin.* 1 John 1:7."[2]

Justice Jackson, of the United States, speaking for the Prosecution, said, in part:

"'The real complaining party at your bar is Civilization. In all our countries it is still a struggling and imperfect thing. It does not plead that the United States, or any other country, has been blameless of the conditions which made the German people easy victims of the blandishments and intimidations of the Nazi conspirators. But it points to the dreadful sequence of aggressions and crimes I have recited, it points to the weariness of flesh, the exhaustion of resources, and the destruction of all that was beautiful or useful in so much of the world, and to greater potentialities for destruction in days to come.'"[3]

But Justice Jackson is wrong. Civilization is not complaining, civilization is not a living being, civilization is but the degree of advancement attained by man in education, culture, science, and religion.

The true complainant is God, and this is what He says, alike to the prisoners at the bar, those sitting in judgment,

[2] G. Morrish, *The Power of the Redeeming Blood* (London: John Wright & Sons Ltd.).
[3] Gilbert, *Nuremberg Diary*, p. 41.

and the world watching this pruning of evil from itself, though the whole tree is basically evil:

(Psalms 2:1)   *Why do the nations rage and the people imagine a vain thing?*

(Isaiah 55:2)   *Wherefore do ye spend money for that which is not bread? and your labour for that which satisfieth not?*

(Isaiah 1:18)   *Come now, and let us reason together, saith the Lord: though your sins be as scarlet, they shall be as white as snow.*

THE APPEAL DECISION

Chapter Eighteen ✠

Saturday, 26th of May, 7 A.M.

Reflections continued to disturb our sleep and to bring us wide awake in the early hours. One could not keep up this pace for long, but it looked as though the end was near.

From the beginning we planned to keep our visits with Adolf Eichmann on a strictly spiritual basis. We wanted to treat him as any other sinner who needs God. We prepared a series of salvation subjects whereby we planned to begin with the fact of man's guilt and proceed to show that Jesus Christ is the only way, but that He is sufficient for the greatest sinner.

We progressed through two thirds of our program and by then came to the conclusion that Eichmann cannot be treated as an ordinary penitent sinner. His complete rejection of any guilt whatsoever left us with no alternative but to enter into a discussion of his past deeds, with a view to bringing to him a sense of guilt.

Through reading books on philosophy, evolution, and other faith-destroying literature he himself "evolved" a god who, though possibly righteous in his estimation, can join in fellowship with evil. He does not express it that way but that would be the logical conclusion of his thinking. Hence there is no need for a "savior," a "mediator," or a Son of God. The Bible was written by man (he claims)—therefore he does not accept it as the word of God and one cannot reason with him on the basis: "it is written."

Whatever his feelings or convictions were while a member of the Nazi Party and especially during the last three years of his activity, by now he has so convinced himself of the complete innocence of his part in the "holocaust" that there is no room in his heart for true repentance. He continually claims that he is free from guilt, that what he did was in execution of orders given him. He claims that he has always been in touch with God, that he prayed every day and even in the midst of the Jewish slaughter. He admits that he made a mistake in joining the Party in the beginning and he regrets what happened as a result of his joining the Party, but that is as far as he will go.

Thus we have no foundation on which to base our talks —he does not believe the Bible. He does not believe that God judges the world; therefore he does not need a savior. He believes that he did right in obeying orders; therefore he has no conviction of sin. Was ever a man in a more hopeless condition?

That is what we started to work on beginning the eleventh of April, 1962. The time was short. The Appeal Court had finished its hearings and was considering its judgment. There was little hope of a favorable verdict.

If we had known in the beginning just what we were dealing with we could have prepared a different approach. But this knowledge could only come day by day as the conversations progressed, and from the letters and treatise he sent us. In the beginning we were not sympathetically moved for the man and hence tried to be as charitable as possible in judging his actions and words. In a measure this helped to dull our perceptions as to the true situation.

Now, forty-five days later, we have the full picture, we believe, and could plan accordingly. But the judgment is only three days away; the time is very short. No reasoned arguments are going to reach the soul of Adolf Eichmann in time. The matter is beyond our help—it is in God's hands. Only a miracle can open the door of his heart and bring a flood of repentance. As we consider the matter we feel that we have been led of God. We persistently have showed him that he is a sinner, as are all men; that Jesus Christ died for his soul and that only through Jesus can he come to God and be saved; that there can be little hope for his life and that he must be prepared to meet God in judgment.

If anything can reach him it can only be the gospel. Reasoned arguments will not do the work. He enjoys nothing better than to explain his ideas of God, but this does not accomplish anything toward his salvation. We believe that God has led us to keep continually chipping away by reiterating the truth concerning Jesus, that He is the only way and his only hope. Nothing but this gospel, quickened by the Holy Spirit, can break down his façade of false innocence, evolutionary theory, and unbelief. Prayer, with a continued witnessing to the truth concerning Jesus Christ, is all that can move him now. He is in the hands of God.

Summary of Eichmann's faith:

1. He believes that there is a God. All nature and the order of the universe prove this to him.

2. He believes that God is absolutely kind and loving.

3. He believes that man is in a process of improvement which will finally result in a perfect man. Animal instincts will disappear as man labors toward perfection.

4. He believes that God is not a God of judgment and punishment, but only of love.

5. He believes that God orders and regulates all things (he calls it fate) and thus he (Eichmann) submits to this.

6. He believes that death is a release of the soul and that this is only another step in the individual's development. He compares the release of the soul with the release of the child's body at birth. Arms, legs, and other members which

were of no use prior to birth become available for use after birth. Thus the soul develops after the death of the body.

All of these ideas came as a result of reading books by men who themselves did not know as much about God as Eichmann did when he started the study.

Tuesday, 29th of May

Today is "judgment day" for Adolf Eichmann. The five members of the Supreme Court of Israel who form the Court of Appeal to hear the appeal of Adolf Eichmann are to give their decision at 9 A.M.

As Mrs. Hull and I entered the "security gate" at Beit Haam we met our friend of many years, Tzvi Terlo, the Assistant Attorney-General, who had done much of the work in preparing the material for the prosecution case. He had a big smile as he remarked to us that my visiting Eichmann was divine irony.

"In all the world," he said, "you were the one Christian clergyman or priest who helped the Hagannah to create the State. Now, out of all the clergymen in the world you are the one who is ministering to Eichmann. It is ironical. *God is laughing at us.*"

9 A.M.

The hall was full when Eichmann came in. He was pale and his face looked as though he had not slept, but he did not look as thin as when we saw him at Ramleh. The glass here must have made a difference. His suit, shirt, and tie possibly made him look fleshier.

The judges filed in immediately when Eichmann was in the court. Without any preliminaries Judge Olshan, the President of the Supreme Court serving as President of this Appeal Court, announced that Justice Agranat would read the first part of the decision.

As the judgment was being read Eichmann sat unmoving, his eyes fixed upon Judge Agranat while he read. His face was expressionless. As reasons justifying the holding of the trial in Israel were mentioned Eichmann looked away from Agranat. His face became stern, hard. He gazed straight ahead.

Judge Agranat read: "He further, contended that also the fact of the appellant's German nationality obliged Israel to follow the course of extraditing him to that state. As to the last fact, let it be said at once that it cannot avail him, as the requirement of making an offer to extradite the offender to the state of his national origin is supported neither by international law nor by the practice of states."

This swept away one hope that Dr. Servatius had expressed to me, beyond a presidential pardon. No wonder Eichmann was stern-looking. He realized the full implications of this decision and was beginning to realize the attitude of the court toward him.

As the court continued to outline the crimes of Eichmann and his main part in handling the "Jewish Question," Eichmann drew down the corners of his mouth. His face flushed red. The judgment was very severe; it did not mince words. Eichmann looked disturbed. His mouth was drawn down again as the words of the judgment tore to shreds his claim rejecting responsibility.

A telegram from Eichmann that had been read in the trial was now read out again: "Eichmann recommends killing by shooting." This was in reference to the Serbian Jews. Eichmann's head went up and back in a defiant manner— the old Nazi still on parade. The court continued to point out that Eichmann was not only interested in transportation but in the actual arrangements for killing as proven by the submitted documents. The judge's remarks were impressive: "No one would have taken him to task, and he would certainly not have been brought to the gallows, had he, to give one example, based himself on the assent of Hitler and Ribbentrop to the emigration to Sweden and Switzerland of a few score thousand of Jews, and had he not undermined it so wickedly and slyly."

The judge continued to say: "Even as there is no word in human speech to designate deeds such as the deeds of the appellant, so there is no punishment in human laws that would fit in its gravity the guilt of the appellant."

. . . *"We have therefore decided to dismiss the appeal both as to the conviction and the sentence, and to affirm the judgment and the sentence of the District Court."*

The end came abruptly, almost unseemly in its haste, considering the seriousness of the judgment given. The judges immediately arose and filed out. Thus ended the appeal of Adolf Eichmann. In its condensation into three and a half hours of the charges made by the prosecuting attorney it was much more stern, more severe, and more devastating than the case originally put by the prosecution counsel.

The session was orderly, the audience respectful, but the reading of the decision, especially the last half, was at a speed that was anything but decorous. The end of the judgment was reached and the court dismissed before anyone was aware it was over.

The audience pushed its way out as though leaving a cinema performance. No one would have expected them to weep tears for the man so soon to die, but at least there could have been a slight hint of solemnity upon the people. The impression one received, however, was that everyone considered it a job well done.

THE THIRTEENTH VISIT

Chapter Nineteen ✠

Thursday, 31st of May

At 1 A.M. this morning the telephone rang. Mrs. Hull answered. A voice asked if I was in, and when asked to wait for me to answer the party closed off. Again at two-thirty this morning there was a ring and inquiry for me. This time we were asked to hold the line. We were under the impression that the Eichmanns, either a brother or Mrs. Eichmann, were trying to reach us from Austria. I held the line for some time. There was a buzzing noise which I presumed came from the overseas operator. After waiting until nearly three o'clock I closed off. There was no further ring.

Later we realized that some ambitious newsman thought that there was a possibility that Eichmann would be hung at that time and if so that I would be at the execution. As long as I was at home he assumed there was no execution. If he reads this he will have the satisfaction of knowing that he kept me up the best part of a night at a time when we were only sleeping about five hours a night and working under great strain. The next night I was to have no sleep at all.

At 8 A.M., as we were about to leave for Ramleh Prison, a call came from Dr. Joseph's secretary. The Minister of Justice wanted to see us that morning. I explained that I had to be at Ramleh at ten and would not have time. It was suggested that we drop in for a moment on the way to Ramleh, to which we agreed.

Dr. Joseph explained to us that in the event that the President did not grant clemency he wanted me to know what the arrangements would be. He questioned whether Mrs. Hull should be subjected to the additional strain of being at the place of execution. There was no thought of her witnessing the hanging, but I would want to talk with the condemned man before his execution and would need an interpreter.

Mrs. Hull assured Dr. Joseph that she would be all right and that she wanted to see the thing through to the end (short of the hanging). "Very well," he said, "I know that you have done social work and possibly this will not be any worse." None of us realized that it might possibly be the only time in history that a woman officially assisted in counseling a condemned man only minutes before his execution.

"You will be given two hours notice," explained Dr. Joseph, "and within that time you must be in Tel Aviv at the address I will give you. There will have to be someone to answer your telephone day and night until the call comes and they will have to be able to contact you within a few minutes. You will meet at this address and from there will be taken in a government car to the place of execution. Four journalists will also be there. The call can come at any time and no notice will be given to the public of the rejection of the plea. The whole matter is strictly confidential."

It was clear that we were approaching the climax. Few realized that the end was actually so near. I thought we might yet have from one to two weeks before an execution would take place.

10:10 A.M.

We arrived at Ramleh Prison ten minutes late due to being detained in Jerusalem. Going up to the death cell I asked the chief warden to arrange for Eichmann to have his Bible and reading glasses for this session. When handed the Bible he said to the chief warden, "I won't need that today."

Eichmann looked different this morning. His face was very hard and his greeting cool. He was not as friendly as usual.

HULL: Are you well?

EICHMANN: Yes, quite well.

HULL: What is your attitude today regarding Jesus Christ?

EICHMANN: Just the same. I have not changed at all.

HULL: Are you still looking to man for hope and pardon?

EICHMANN: Man does not interest me. I do not care what he thinks. I am not guilty of the things charged against me. The greatest part of what was said in court was not true.

MRS. HULL: The court session must have been very hard for you.

EICHMANN: No, it was not hard. I cannot be responsible for all that is said about me.

HULL: Are you resigned to your fate?

EICHMANN: Yes, I am quite prepared to die.

HULL: Won't you let us help you to further prepare?

EICHMANN: What is the use of discussing it? I wrote three letters to you and everything is plainly given in those letters. You have not answered them and will not discuss them. (He did not realize the length of time necessary for his letter to go through security and then for his difficult handwriting and involved thinking in German to be deciphered and studied before we could reply. There had not been time for this prior to our previous visit and this was our first visit in a full week. As the interview progressed we realized that he was very resentful because of the Appeal Court's review of his acts and its decision to reject his appeal. We had to bear the brunt of this.)

HULL: I have prepared a letter for you (I show it to him through the glass) which is an answer to your three letters. It will be given to you after we leave.

EICHMANN: Thank you.

HULL: The only comfort we can bring you is from the Bible.

EICHMANN: I am not interested in Jewish stories.

HULL: It is not stories we want you to read but what God has spoken.

EICHMANN: What I believe I wrote you. I made it very clear. I am not interested in anything else. There is no point or purpose in discussing anything else.

HULL: Then what is the point of my being here?

EICHMANN: The sentence was clear. I am going to be hung. Why should I pretend to believe something I don't believe?

HULL: Haven't you given any thought as to what will be your end?

EICHMANN: It means nothing to me.

HULL: But you are going to hell!

EICHMANN: I do not believe in hell. Those are men's thoughts; there is no hell.

HULL: You make it very hard and difficult for us. God help you. Your wife believes as we do; why are you so opposed?

EICHMANN: There is no purpose in your telling me what you believe; everything is quite clear. I am satisfied with my ideas. I know that I am going to die—in two weeks, or two days, or one day. I am not interested in making a show of confession before men.

HULL: It would not be a show before men, but rather before God. We are trying to help you get ready to meet God.

EICHMANN: You cannot do that through the Bible. I am ready through my philosophy. I am ready for everything. I am very happy and contented and I am not ready to accept anything in the Bible or any different ideas from what I now believe.

HULL: We have come to visit you thirteen times because we wanted to help you. This may be the last time we will have an opportunity to talk with you. (We did not realize how true this was.) As a favor to us, won't you read three or four passages from the Bible?

EICHMANN: Don't tell me that you came thirteen times for me. You did not do me any favor. I wrote you in the beginning—

MRS. HULL: But—

EICHMANN: (rudely) Don't interrupt me. Let me talk. I wrote you right at the start what I believed and you need not have come. I am under no obligation to you.

HULL: We know that, yet we wish you would read some verses with us.

EICHMANN: No, I won't read the Bible. I have my own thoughts and I am preparing my way and have no time to read and discuss your way and your ideas. I do not want to take time now with other ideas; there would be no purpose in it.

HULL: Does it mean nothing to you that millions of Christians are praying for your salvation?

EICHMANN: I can't change my ideas because people are praying. What benefit would it be if I were a hypocrite and said that I believe when I don't believe?

HULL: We don't want you to be a hypocrite. We only want you to give God a chance.

EICHMANN: God has spoken to me and leads me. You don't know whether you are right. Possibly I *am* making a mistake, but possibly you are wrong. We won't know who is right until after death. I feel that I am in contact with God through my belief.

HULL: Did you know that Dr. Hans Frank repented at Nuremberg?

EICHMANN: Yes, I heard that he repented, but he was guilty. He was a general, he gave the commands and orders. He needed to repent, but I am not guilty. (He was insulted that we compared him with Dr. Frank.)

HULL: It was not that he repented for what he did so much as the fact that he prepared himself to meet God.

EICHMANN: I read something about his repentance, but only a part of it. But I do not take him as an example.

HULL: Frank made himself ready to meet God.

EICHMANN: I am not responsible for the things I am charged with. I am ready to meet God. Frank merely went back to the church he left. He lost contact and then came back to it again.

HULL: We do not want you to come back to the Church but to accept Jesus Christ as your Saviour.

EICHMANN: I do not need a middleman or mediator. I go directly to God myself. I am very dogmatic on this, so I don't believe in Jesus Christ.

HULL: Are you still praying?

EICHMANN: I will not answer that question. With these microphones everyone can hear what is said, so I will not discuss that now.

HULL: We, too, regret the necessity of the microphones but there is nothing we can do about it.

EICHMANN: *When we come to the end I might have something different to say.*

HULL: We will be with you all the way to the end.

EICHMANN: It is not necessary for you to trouble yourself that way unless you wish.

HULL: We do wish and will come until the end. We believe that even yet God can reach your heart.

EICHMANN: *At the last I will tell everything when it will not be in public as here.* (This opportunity never arose prior to the execution.) A good friend of mine in Argentina asked me whether I was going to die with my present belief or whether I would come back to the Christian faith. That was some years ago. I told him that I could not answer then but must wait until it came time for me to die. No man knows in what faith he will die. I believe that I will die in my present belief, but this I cannot know yet.

HULL: Do you remember what we told you ten days ago? When in need, when desperate, call on the name of Jesus. All power in heaven and in earth is in that name.

EICHMANN: (no answer)

HULL: Please study and give consideration to the letter we are leaving for you. We will come again until the end.

EICHMANN: I see that the Christians are very concerned about how I will die. Why are they so disturbed? For me, I am not concerned; my religion does not make me upset like that.

HULL: We are concerned for the one whom we think is not ready to die or to meet God. We are not concerned for ourselves.

MRS. HULL: Even your wife is concerned, if she believes as you say she does. She is just as concerned for your soul as we are.

EICHMANN: She knows that I am not guilty. She is not concerned.

HULL: We are not concerned about your guilt but as to whether you are ready to meet God. Your wife knows that Jesus is the door, that the only way is through that door. You are lost unless you come through the door.

EICHMANN: I do not believe that, because man wrote that.

HULL: No, Jesus said that.

MRS. HULL: How blind can you be? We are praying that God will open your eyes and take that blindness away. The world has not been so kind to you. Why don't you prepare yourself for heaven? Heaven is such a beautiful place where you will be with God. You can only get there through Jesus Christ. He is the door and you have to go through that door or you are lost and will go to hell.

EICHMANN: Yes, this world does not interest me. I have nothing to live for here, but I have my belief. I am ready to die and I do not want to be upset now. I can honestly say that I am prepared to die. You are concerned for me because of what you heard in court on Tuesday.

HULL: No, we would talk to any man this way. Anyone who does not believe in Jesus is not ready to die.

MRS. HULL: When I write my children, my son and my

daughters, I ask them, too, whether they are ready to die and meet God. I ask them if they were in an accident would they be ready to die. We are concerned for any human being who is going to die—is he ready through Jesus Christ to meet God? Even the policemen here, they are not guilty of anything, but if I had the opportunity I would ask them if they were ready to meet God through Jesus Christ.

EICHMANN: I would not accept that. If you could hear me talk to my God you would find that I have peace.

HULL: There is no more that we can do for you today but pray that God will make you to know that Jesus is the way and that there is no other way but through Him. Please read the letter we are leaving for you.

EICHMANN: Yes I will.

HULL: *Auf Wiedersehen.*

EICHMANN: *Auf Wiedersehen.*

Going downstairs, the chief warden said: "I could only wish that when I am about to die I would have the same opportunity as you have given him. It is wonderful the patience you have had. He was so insulted when you compared him to Frank."

EICHMANN'S THIRD LETTER

Chapter Twenty ✠

On our eighth visit to Eichmann, Sunday, the thirteenth of May, we had left a questionnaire which we had asked him to answer with a thesis of five or six pages. The questionnaire was as follows:

Would you please write us a short thesis in letter form on:

1. What you believe about God.
2. How you found God in nature.
3. On what you base your hope for a future life after death.

He replied to our questions on the fifteenth of May. The paper went to Tel Aviv for examination and was handed to us on our tenth visit, Sunday, May 20. As usual the translation of his document was a difficult task, both from the standpoint of handwriting and meaning. I studied the translation and prepared an answer to it on May 27. Our first visit to Eichmann after this date was the thirty-first of May, for the appeal decision came in between.

Eichmann's letter, when translated, read as follows:

Dear Reverend Mr. Hull,

You asked me three questions and I will try to answer them.

A. "How did you find God in nature and what do you believe about God?"

I will reply briefly:

1. Concerning the earth, through seeing the causes and their results.

(For instance the *position* and *relation* of the earth to the sun.)

Cause: Her own rotation, the movement around the sun, the angle between the supposed axis of the earth and its inclination, the atmospheric veil.

Effect: The sequence of the seasons and the changes of climates, which in turn are the

Causes of the circulation of water and air, from which, again, the

Result is the differences of temperature, bringing about decay and growth which lead Goethe to coin his maxim, Stirb und Werde [Die and be born]! This is the

Cause for development of life on our earth, and one of the

Results, according to uncounted studies, is, for instance, the existence and development of man. Only a planning *power* could accomplish this.

2. *The very tiny worlds, the atomic ones,* put us into awed amazement by the precision of their planned order, and this planning power gives me the idea that this planning power of order *must* be the power that *created* as well.

I have been in the Urania observatory in Vienna. I have lain many nights under the starry sky of the south. I have been on top of the high Mt. El Ponchude in the north of Argentina and have observed

3. *Our own universe* and the Milky Way. Also, through the telescope I have watched the farthest galaxies that appear to us as mere patches of mist.

4. *The nebula of the far galaxies.*

5. *I read* the books of physicists, astronomers and philosophers. *I think, I compare, I seek* for cause and effect. I have concerned myself with the rise and fall of the galaxies. I am interested in the methods of *radioactive dating* and the opportunities this opens up for measuring and development of our own world. I am deeply interested in the words Pope Pius XII spoke a few years before his death at a meeting of scientists in the Vatican. On that occasion the Pope, who was as cautious as he was wise, said in effect that he "did not refuse" to recognize that *the beginning of time* may have happened about ten billions of years ago.

(According to radioactive dating it was five billion years ago.) I have learned that, as early as ten years ago, it was possible to look into space to a distance of 1000 million light years. I know that even within this limited distance there are millions of milky ways and in them billions of suns with trillions of planets. If you multiply 9½ billions a billion times, you get the total distance in kilometers in which man may look into space.

Then I must consider that this distance compared to eternity (which I understand does have a measurable end after all) is about as great as the depth of a coal mine compared to the diameter of the whole earth; when I furthermore realize that there is no *proof* that beyond this immense space there are no further spaces —when to comprehend all this, I must think of the construction of the atomic worlds—then I am left in amazement and awe before this *gigantic, regulating, planning, creating* power that *directs* the movements of the tiniest, as well as the greatest worlds. And *this is God!*

The Free Masons have aptly described this power as "the Architect of all Worlds." What is man with all his knowledge and will compared to this almightiness of God? Less than a drop of water in all the waters of the world.

For *me* all this is *proof of the existence of God.* For me, this means not only belief in this power without actual knowledge of God, it means *knowing* that God exists and believing in him. As I study the cosmic laws, I recognize in the order of movement and in the order of creation the *absolute goodness* of this regulating power. A power that cannot possibly—and now I turn to man's place in the world-order—have created us men to spend our days of life in fear and suffering. *Otherwise* this kind power would never have implanted in man the will of the individual to change, it could not have endowed us with the will to goodness as an essential, driving force of man's innermost self. Certainly, *this* is what Spinoza had in mind when he said that in this world there exists nothing that is evil in itself. And Kant spoke of our *inborn* duty to realize ethical values; man's inherited law of morality.

Dear Reverend, I see you smiling at my words and I hear your wife asking me again, why then are you here? I must answer that one should consider not only the judicial judgment, the publicity given to the accusations against me, but also the defense of my advocate, oral and written, and my own words in the court. It was Kant who stated that when it comes to the *realization* of ethics, governments may become obstacles.

Man, a product of development willed by the Creator, is still in the early stages of becoming, only on the way toward perfection.

One of my brothers wrote me in April: "Why and for what purpose was your fate drawn like this?" He asked me what is the purpose of life, whether life is worth living. He cannot find any purpose in my life, nor make sense of it. I answered him on nine pages, as well as I could. Here are some extracts from my answer:

"Man as a species is still young; our entire universe is not yet old. There is still egoism, envy, bad instincts. But these are being ground away in the process of development and are being replaced by charity, peace and joy. Some philosophers—" so I went on—"think that later more perfect generations may even move on from the love of their neighbors to love of those farthest away as a goal of ethics. War and destruction will disappear through man's development toward goodness and become relics of a dark past. Surely," so I went on in my letter, "it must be our task to struggle against our lower instincts, because the sum of innumerable thoughts of generations shape the reality."

Today one must ask what good we can derive from all the ideals of a Socrates or a Plato as long as governments can force their citizens against their will for doing good to murder and to exterminate. None of this applies to me! I was constantly asking for a transfer; I have one of those documents right here. All my requests were declined, usually on the grounds of war regulations.

Furthermore I wrote to my brother, "One is certainly justified in asking oneself, what is the good of all this; what is the higher sense of our lives; what is right and what is justice? What is the meaning of all these transcendent conceptions such as honor, fidelity, right and so on? And as seen from a lower point of view, it can really drive one to despair." Then, in effect, I told my brother all the things I told you on the previous pages. I added that my *inner ego* is the total of all the experiences and thoughts of my ancestors, plus my own small experience. This is *my thinking*, the spiritual part of me. That is the truly *human—the uniqueness*. From generation to generation it becomes more perfect.

Our former animal instincts will disappear by our own efforts within ourselves. But *human* development toward perfection must be measured not in generations but in aeons.

I am just a small part of the total; only a small link in an endlessly long chain. I have the task to pass on with love and care that which has been entrusted to me (the spiritual values) *so that it will continue to develop toward perfection.* The eternal track of love carries this on, according to the will of the Creator. This for me is the higher sense of my existence as a human being. In my conception God, *because of his almightiness,* is not a punisher, not an angry God, but rather an all-embracing God in whose order I have been placed. And his order (fate) regulates everything. All being and becoming—including me—is *subject* to this order. Thus I have tried, very briefly, to answer your questions one and two.

B. "On what do you base your hope for a future life after death?"

Even the human body consists of only matter and energy. The spirit within me, my inner being, are my thoughts and my feelings. In my opinion these are energy. According to the law of nature, no energy will be lost. Matter is subjected to an eternal change; energy *may* be changed. There is no fixed being, there is no rest, there is no nothingness; (there is also no "death.") "Everything is in flux," said the ancient and say the modern philosophers. *The end of the human being is the birth of the soul.* This is a *logical development toward further perfection,* it is only another, further *step in the development of being.* This form of development *must,* according to my logic (in regard to the natural law) *gradually lead to a form higher than the human being.* For me this is another manifestation of the *greatness of the divine creative will.*

If someone should come back from the "beyond" to give us a report on the world of the souls it would cause mankind to commit suicide. Doubtless man is the first step in the development of the soul, a divine order of creation. Who will prove to me that it is not so? *I believe* in my conception. And thereby I have answered your question number three on which my hope for a future life is based. Again this is *only a sketch.* (However, I would like to amend your question concerning the word "hope" and to put instead the definitive word "conception" or "belief.")

Dear pastor, you asked me to answer on five or six pages; thus I have reached my limit.

Let me just take the opportunity here to tell you openly, respected Mr. Hull, that your answer to my *last* note on six pages did *not* satisfy me; or did you not wish to enter into discussion of the problems I wrote about? If that is so, I will consider the case closed.

With sincere greetings,

Signed: Adolf Eichmann

15-5-62

Written from Ramleh Prison.

The following letter was written in reply to the above and the previous letter. It was taken to Ramleh Prison on our thirteenth visit, Thursday, 10 A.M., the thirty-first of May, and shown to Eichmann through the glass. I told him that the prison authorities would give it to him after I left, and asked him to read and study it. As it developed, there was no time for the letter to be passed by security and returned to Ramleh before the execution took place. This was *the letter that never was read:*

ZION CHRISTIAN MISSION

Jerusalem   Israel

27th of May, 1962

Mr. Adolf Eichmann,

You mentioned in your last letter that you were not satisfied with my answers to your previous letter. I will explain why I did not discuss it with you at greater length.

Your ideas, as you had previously pointed out to us both in your first letter and in our conversations, are very far from the Gospel of Jesus Christ. On studying your letter I came to the conclusion that you were not yet aware of the imminence of death. Such ideas as you had might satisfy one for a time while living under normal conditions and with a normal expectancy of life. But such ideas must pass away as a morning mist when one is brought face to face with death. Please read Isaiah 28:17, *Judgment . . . and the hail shall sweep away the refuge of lies.* Again in Isaiah 28:20, *For the bed is shorter than that a man can stretch himself on it: and the covering narrower than that he can wrap himself in it.* Your "bed" of philosophy is too short, it is all man's reasoning; and your evolutionary ideas of progress to perfection by man is too narrow a "covering" when you will come face to face with God.

Because we were concerned for the salvation of your soul, and in view of the brief time we had left in which to minister to you we felt it more important to deal with spiritual truths as we see them rather than to enter into a discussion of the views you hold. Your treatise has explained your views and enlarged our understanding of them and we briefly reply herewith. This letter is an answer to all your letters, including the last treatise on your ideas of God and your future hope after death.

You state that you believe that there is a God because all nature and the cosmic order of the universe prove it to you. I agree with this one hundred percent, and the Bible also confirms this thought. Psalms, Chapter 8, 147, and 148, Romans, Chapter 1.

Then you say that you recognize the absolute kindness of God and that God would not have created man to live all his days in fear and suffering. True, God is kind and loving and no man needs to live in fear and suffering. I do not live in fear and suffering, no man needs to, for Jesus Christ died to deliver us from fear and suffering. You are now living in fear and suffering because you rejected Jesus Christ. If you had held to the faith of your childhood and not entered into the philosophic thoughts of Spinoza and Kant you could now be living a happy normal life.

You blame governments for your present position. What is a government? It is not a building of stone, with rooms and office furniture and files. A government is made up of people, some of whom believe as you do, others believe as I do, some have no faith at all. It is not the building which makes the law, it is the minds of the people. I challenge you to show me one real born-again Christian with true faith in Jesus Christ who would pass the Nuremberg Laws or endorse the actions and policies of the Nazi Party. These things were the acts of men who had rejected Jesus Christ. You say that priests and ministers, Protestant ministers, blessed the armies and acts of Nazi Germany. I say, they may have had priestly robes or clerical gowns but they definitely were not true followers of the Lord Jesus Christ.

You ask, What has Christianity done with all its remedy to make a change? I do not answer that question because it refers to a movement which is Christian in name only and not in acts. Read what so-called Christianity did in Spain, in Rome, and throughout Europe through the centuries of time. Read how so-called Christians tortured and killed Jews, Protestants and anyone else who did not follow the prescribed rules and beliefs of the moment.

I do not preach Christianity, I preach Jesus Christ. If you will ask me what Jesus Christ has done to change the world then I will wax eloquent and tell you of how He saved me, a sinner. I can tell you how He changed my life. I can tell you of how He took all fear from my heart and in place of it put a joy and happiness and a looking forward to that day when I shall see Him face to face. What a glorious day that will be for me when I see Jesus. That is what He has done for me and what He can do for you.

You claim that man is still being developed and progressing unto perfection. It is too bad that you have been out of touch with this world for the last two years. One has only to look at it today to see what a hopeless condition man has created on earth. Getting better? If this is better then let me go to the hell that this world progressed from. I am afraid that the progression has been at the rate of one step forward and two backwards until now man has reached the brink and is about to plunge this whole world into utter chaos.

You claim that God is not an angry God and not a punisher. In other words you do not believe that God is the judge of all the earth. You claim that your soul will be released at death and be free. This, you say, is your belief and you ask, Who will prove that it is *not* so? I ask you, What proof have you that it *is* so?

I have told you that your time on earth is short. You are soon going to have an answer to this question for you will be brought before an almighty God and then you will find out that it is *not* so. Then you will find out your mistake—but it will be too late.

Adolf Eichmann, I have told you that no man on earth can prove to you the error of your ideas, nor the truth of what the Bible says. But God can and will do both these now if you will let Him. Let God speak to your heart. Throw overboard your own ideas. Read the word of God and believe. Accept Jesus Christ now as your Saviour and be saved. THIS IS YOUR ONLY HOPE.

Sincerely yours,

Signed: (Rev.) William L. Hull

THE EXECUTION

Chapter Twenty-one ✠

Thursday, 31st of May, 7:50 P.M.

We had just completed the transcript of the morning session in Ramleh. The telephone rang.

DR. JOSEPH: You have two hours to be in Tel Aviv. You are put on your honor not to divulge anything until the end of the matter.

HULL: Of course. Do I have any ministerial duties in connection with the body after the execution? I mean as at a funeral.

DR. JOSEPH: No.

We left Jerusalem at 8:30 P.M. and arrived in Tel Aviv at 9:50 P.M. The assembly point was to be at the prison doctor's house. The others who were to meet there were all from Tel Aviv and were there ahead of us. There were four journalists to represent the press, the doctor, several police and security men, and the district officer from Ramleh. We left the rendezvous at 10:00 P.M. I had been told that I would have to leave my car in Tel Aviv, so I parked it near the government press office and drove with the others in a government car. Our destination had not been revealed. Even the driver of the car did not know his final destination. The press was speculating as to where the execution would take place. They suggested various spots, but I felt that it would be right at Ramleh Prison, as too much would be involved in moving Eichmann and providing security.

As the car sped out of Tel Aviv we did not head for the direct road to Ramleh Prison but rather to the Jerusalem-Tel Aviv road. We drove some distance toward Jerusalem and then stopped just past the Rehovot road. Our driver parked off the road and waited for further instructions. A car drove up and a man jumped out and whispered to the driver of our car. Again we moved on in the direction of Jerusalem until we arrived at the Ramleh town police station.

We all disembarked here. The journalists waited but Mrs. Hull and I were put into another car and driven on, finally arriving at Ramleh Prison where we had been only that morning. A police vehicle was blocking the road leading to the north gate. It was filled with police, and after being examined our car was permitted to pass on. Arriving at the prison we were taken immediately to Eichmann's cell. As we came to the top of the stairs we noticed that the wall opposite the door to the death cell had been broken down, leaving an entrance through to the rest of the floor. I thought to myself that they might have left this until after the execution.

We entered the cell at 11:20 P.M.

HULL: *Guten abend.*

EICHMANN: *Guten abend.* You look very sad. Why are you sad? I am not sad.

HULL: We *are* sad, because we know that your end is at hand. We kept warning you that it was near. Now it has come. But if you repent we will not be sad. Have you changed any in your attitude since this morning? Are you sorry for what you have done? Are you ready to repent?

EICHMANN: No, I have not changed my mind. I am quite settled in my mind.

HULL: When were you told that the end is at hand?

EICHMANN: Just a short time ago, about two hours. I was very astonished that they rushed things as they did in the appeal and now. But I have peace in my heart. In fact I am astonished that I have such peace. When I consider the peace I have I say to myself how wonderful is my belief that it should give me such peace. Death frightens most people but not me, for I know that I am right in believing as I told you in our discussions, that death is but the release of the soul. In our discussions I mentioned how natural birth is parallel with the soul's release at death. There is a design in nature which shows a plan with everything in order. It can't be anything else. (He continued to talk of his God in nature, as many times before.) You are so sad and concerned about death but you see that I am not. (His face lit up with a big smile.)

CHIEF WARDEN: (to us) I have to limit your time. You have five minutes more.

HULL: (to Eichmann) We are sad because of your spiritual condition.

MRS. HULL: You are blind and you won't let God show you. I am here as in the place of your wife and you are so full of pride and want so much to make a good showing at the end that you do not even consider your wife and children, your little Haasi, and what they will have to try and live down because of the life you have led. You know how much they will suffer. If you would repent and let the world see that you are sorry for what you have done and accept the Lord Jesus Christ as your Saviour, people would have more compassion for your family. You are a very selfish and proud man.

EICHMANN: (very excitedly) *Nein, Nein.* I am not proud. That is one thing I am not. I am not proud.

CHIEF WARDEN: (to us) Don't get him too excited.

MRS. HULL: Our time is very short so listen very carefully. This is the last we have to say, we have to leave you. Remember the thief on the cross. At the last minute he repented on the cross and asked Jesus to remember him when He would come into His Kingdom. At the last minute, maybe, you will change your mind and want to get into this Kingdom too, instead of going to hell.

HULL: Call on the name of Jesus.

MRS. HULL: Yes, call on the name of Jesus. All power in heaven and earth is in that name.

EICHMANN: Is the Reverend going with me to the end?

MRS. HULL: Yes, to the very end.

HULL: Do you have any special message you wish us to give to your wife and family?

EICHMANN: I wrote my brother and my wife this afternoon but tell my wife that I took it calmly and that I had peace in my heart, which guarantees to me that I am right.

HULL: Would you like us to send the German Bible we gave you to your wife?

EICHMANN: No, she has her own.

MRS. HULL: But maybe she would like the one you used for the last few weeks of your life.

EICHMANN: Yes, that would be nice. Please send it to her.

We left then at 11:40 P.M. Mrs. Hull went down to the warden's office. I remained in the chief warden's office in the death cell apartment while Eichmann was being prepared for execution.

Eichmann strongly maintained that he was ready to die with peace in his heart. He persisted in his belief to the end of our discussions. He gave every appearance of being happy, even cheerful, and with no sign of fear. He appeared to welcome the end. As I sat in the office a prison guard came in for another cupful of dry white wine for Eichmann, who had already had several and seemed to be slightly affected by the wine. Yet, when the chief warden came to tie his wrists and put on handcuffs, he asked for one minute in which to pray.

This was granted to him and he stood in the corner and prayed. Then he turned to the chief warden and said, "I am ready." I never learned what he prayed.

11:55 P.M.

All is in readiness. I was called. Eichmann, with his hands tied behind his back, handcuffed to a guard on each side, stood in the center of the room where the cubicle was. For the first time I saw Eichmann without glass between us. He smiled at me.

The chief warden said to me: "You lead the way please. Go straight down the corridor." I turned and started out the cell. Now it was evident why the wall had been broken through, as we noticed on our way in to our last visit with Eichmann. It made a way to the far end of what was the third floor of the building.

We crossed the stair landing, passed through the opening in the wall, and went straight down the corridor.

The chief warden called to me: "Slower please."

Halfway, Eichmann stopped and asked a guard to wipe his nose. One took a handkerchief out of Eichmann's breast pocket and wiped his nose. We then proceeded. Eichmann seemed to stagger a little but was firmly held by his two guards.

As we started again a guard called from the end of the corridor to wait, that it was not ready. What a gruesome situation: the prisoner behind me swaying between his two guards, all ready for his execution and his executioners not ready for him.

The chief warden called back that it had to be ready and ordered us to continue on. My watch showed 11:59 P.M.

We came to the door at the end of the corridor and I stepped to one side and Eichmann was taken in. I then went into the adjoining room where the four pressmen and some police and government officials were waiting. I was there but one minute when I was called to come into the execution room. Eichmann was standing in the middle of the room. A hole had been cut in the floor and a wooden platform now filled this hole. The platform was level with the floor.

Eichmann stood on this platform. A heavy rope was coiled above his head and fastened to an iron frame. I stood in front of Eichmann, but two or three feet from him. I said to him: *"Jesus, Jesus, Herr Jesus, mein Heiland"*—*"Jesus, Jesus, Lord Jesus, my Saviour."* He looked at me but gave no recognition or awareness of what I said. The press were called in. They crowded in together with the officials. They stood beside me and along the side of the room on the right hand of Eichmann. The reporters immediately began to write, noting all details. There was a metal lever two feet high and with a handle protruding from the floor on my right hand. It was partly covered by a curtain hanging on a wire and extending outward from the wall behind me. The guards were busy strapping his legs and arms.

Eichmann called out in German:

"Long live Germany. Long live Argentina. Long live Austria.

"These are the three countries with which I have been most connected and which I will not forget. I greet my wife, my family, and my friends. I had to obey the laws of war and my flag. I am ready."

Later:

"Gentlemen, we shall meet again soon, so is the fate of all men. I have believed in God all my life and I die believing in God."

Eichmann refused the black hood. The guard threw it over by me.

The guards then took the rope, which had a large noose in it, and prepared it to put over Eichmann's head. Even at this point the above-ordinary kindness which had been shown this prisoner by the police was evident. The rope was one and a half inches thick and the guards had wrapped a piece of rubber around the noose part of the rope so that it would not cut Eichmann's throat.

The noose was doubled and put over Eichmann's head. The two thicknesses of rope formed a high tight collar around his neck and he had to hold his head high. I continued to urge him to call on the name of Jesus. He ignored me. I bowed my head in prayer; I would not look on the final act.

"*Mouchan!*" (Ready)

"*Paal!*" (Action)

Friday, 1st of June, 12:02 A.M.

The lever was pulled giving a loud clang, the platform dropped, and Eichmann fell to the end of the rope, a distance of about ten feet. The reporter on my left leaned forward to look down the hole. I could not look. It was both awesome and weird. No one spoke or moved except the reporter. All that could be heard was a drip, drip on the floor below. Then we slowly went out. I had no special feelings. I was benumbed. A great sadness filled me that a soul had rejected God's great salvation and gone to hell. *For God so loved the world, that he gave his only begotten Son, that whosoever believeth in him should not perish, but have everlasting life.*

In the whole life of Eichmann there is nothing that one could point out to admire or respect. He was a weakling who was willing to serve his superiors regardless of the immorality of their demands. Yet at the last moment, the eyewitnesses had to admit, he died courageously. He did not break down, he did not weaken. How much of his courage was due to the white wine he drank prior to his execution will never be known, but this one thing was clear: he died boldly.

I went downstairs with Mr. Nir and the others. Mrs. Hull was waiting in one of the offices. There was a cup of coffee in front of her, untouched. She told me later that when I had come in, both Mr. Nir and I were deathly white.

The four pressmen wanted to question me about my last conversation with Eichmann. I answered some of their questions. When finished I asked Mr. Nir about the Bible for Mrs.

Eichmann. A reporter leaned over to hear, so Mr. Nir said he would discuss it later. He told me that he would appreciate it if Mrs. Hull would let a police car take her home to Jerusalem and I would remain. They would need me for several hours if I were willing to wait. I agreed and went back to Mrs. Hull. She and Mr. Nir's secretary were the only two women in the building, except the women prisoners.

At first Mrs. Hull was inclined to wait for me, as long as Mrs. Epstein remained. Later she agreed to go when Mr. Nir pointed out to her that it would be a wait of many hours.

12:45 A.M.

When the white police station wagon was ready Mrs. Epstein and I escorted Mrs. Hull to the north gate of the compound. There were several cars outside on the road and when her car was located she went out the gate. We returned to the prison.

Mrs. Hull later informed me that from the moment the car left the prison gate police security measures were evident. The road to Ramleh was closed off. At the point where the prison road joined the Ramleh road an open troop carrier filled with police, all armed, stood on guard. The car had to stop and be checked by police with flashlights. About every five hundred yards armed police with flashlights were posted. A mounted motorcycle policeman turned when her car failed to stop for identification and overtook and stopped the car.

On the Ramleh road where it joined the Tel Aviv-Jerusalem highway another open troop carrier was parked, filled with armed police. One hundred yards in front of this was a metal carpet four feet wide and filling the road from side to side. It was made up of several strips of metal in which were set steel spikes about five inches high and about five inches apart. To drive over these would wreck every tire. In order for Mrs. Hull's car to pass, these strips were moved. They were in two sections and had to be switched around to leave room for the car to go through. At the lorry the car was again checked and passed. From then on, while traveling on the road to Jerusalem, there were frequent checks by armed police with flashlights. The two police accompanying Mrs. Hull were both well armed and went with her to our apartment to check and make sure everything was safe there. She arrived in Jerusalem at 3 A.M.

ASHES TO ASHES—
DUST TO DUST

Chapter Twenty-two ✠

Friday, 1st of June, 1 A.M.

Mr. Nir came and asked me to accompany him. He took me into the next office, that of the warden, where we had so many times discussed the problem of the unrepentant Eichmann. Four paper forms were on the desk and I was asked to put my signature on them as witness to the execution. Asking whether to sign in English or Hebrew I was told it did not matter. I signed in Hebrew characters as the others had signed.

The pressmen were leaving as Mr. Nir and I, accompanied by several policemen, also went out of the prison. We used the back door, which took us out through the staff quarters outside. It was brightly lighted everywhere and there was much activity and many police around. The whole prison was alerted and stirred.

At the north gate of the compound we waited until the press had gone out and then a party of eight or ten of us, led by Mr. Nir, walked down the road past the front of the prison toward the south gate. We went out the gate and at a distance of one hundred yards passed a police lorry and many police guarding the road. In but a moment we turned left onto a dirt track which led through a grove of trees.

In the grove we heard a great deal of shouting, and there were bright lights. A short distance down the track we came to a police guard with a large electric lantern. Its bright rays identified us and we again turned left and entered the grove itself. There were police trucks and pickups around and many men standing about. Others seemed very busy. A four-inch fire hose lay across our path.

I was taken through the crowd and on the left could see a bright fire and hear a very loud roar. The crowd of police parted for Mr. Nir and myself and we approached what seemed a great oven standing five feet high, about three feet wide, and seven feet long. The top was rounded and on the front was an iron door hinged at the top and operated by a lever on the side.

Facing the front of the oven was a two-pronged metal fork about twelve feet long. The prongs were steel, about three or four inches thick. This metal arrangement was sitting on a metal track which came out from the oven.

Lying on the two metal prongs was what looked like a body wrapped in gray woolen blankets. Mr. Nir asked me to identify the body. I asked for the face covering to be removed. The blanket was pulled back and the face revealed it to be the body of Adolf Eichmann. I indicated my identification and the face was covered again. The oven door opened and a blazing inferno was revealed within.

The order was given for the body to be pushed into the crematorium, but as the metal prongs holding the body were moved forward the body became unbalanced and fell off on the ground. It seemed almost indecent to look upon the scene as the blanket fell away, again exposing the face and body. With some difficulty the body was restored to its place on the metal prongs. The heat must have been terrific for the men, for the oven door was still open, the fire raging within. We thought of the scene in Daniel where the king *commanded that they should heat the furnace one seven times more than it was wont to be heated.*

Eventually the metal prongs holding the body were

pushed into the furnace and the body held there while the prongs were withdrawn. Then the door clanged shut and great billows of black smoke poured out the ten-foot chimney at the far end of the oven. What a strange fate for one who had sent so many to the same strange death, but they were not strengthened and fortified by wine. Rather, they were burned alive. Slowly we retraced our steps to the prison. One felt too numb to really think the thing out.

In the warden's office soft drinks were provided. About six police officials and a civilian, the Ramleh district officer, sat around in the office, with others coming and going.

One of them, a captain, was handsome enough to be in Hollywood. In his summer uniform, with his sleeves rolled up, his tattooed numbers from the German concentration camp could easily be read. I looked at the blue numbers and thought of God's promise to Israel: *No weapon that is forged against thee shall prosper.* This man—he must have been quite young in Nazi days—was one of those who signed as witness to the execution and subsequent details of the disposal of the body of Adolf Eichmann.

There seemed to be a feeling of relief that everything was over, but there was no hilarity. We sat around and waited; occasionally one would reminisce on some aspect of Eichmann's detention. I queried the chief warden as to where Eichmann had been exercised and was surprised to find out that it had been on the open roof of the building in broad daylight and in full view of traffic which passed on the road east of the prison.

The paper forms testifying to the identification of the body before cremation were again brought in to be signed. I suggested to Mr. Nir that it would be better, possibly, if I signed in English so as to establish the fact to the world that a non-Jew was present throughout. He agreed, so I signed in English and Mr. Nir had the first papers brought also so that I might re-sign them in English.

Mr. Nir had gone out but came back at about 2:30 A.M. He told us that everything would be ready in a few minutes.

I gained fresh respect for Mr. Nir that night and the next few days, too, as the full details of the security measures became known. Everything, both the execution and subsequent events, as well as security, was handled expertly and without much fuss, yet this was the first hanging in the fourteen years of the history of the state.

At 2:50 a call came on the telephone and it was announced that all was ready. Once again we went out the south gate to the scene of the cremation. The picture was different now. There were less men about and fewer lights. No longer did the fire roar and shine brightly. All was quiet and dark.

Again we approached the furnace. The front was opened. A small pile of ashes had been raked up to the front. Sparks were still flying about in the oven, like fireflies. A large black pan, two feet long, twelve inches wide, and four inches deep was held against the stove and the ashes scraped into it. Mr. Nir had brought a small nickled can, almost like a milk pail, about two gallons in size. It had a lid which fitted tightly into the top, and a swing handle.

Carefully the ashes were poured into the pail until the pan had been emptied of every vestige of ash. Then the cover was put on firmly and from that time on Mr. Nir never let the pail out of his hand.

Someone had indicated that the ashes were to be scattered on the sea. Mr. Nir's car was waiting. It was approximately 3 A.M. The Ramleh district officer and I rode in the back seat, Mr. Nir in the front beside the driver with the pail between his feet. At the junction with the Tel Aviv-Jerusalem highway security measures were still evident, although it could be seen that the police were preparing to leave. The lorry full of armed police was still there and on the crossroad another police vehicle was parked. Behind this was a small foreign car, evidently held there by the police. A lady was in the front seat and as our white car passed the police car and turned sharply right into the Tel Aviv-Jerusalem road she put her head out the window facing us to identify us. The man who was in the driver's seat jumped out and ran around his car toward ours as we gathered speed after the turn. He was still twenty feet away as our car passed him and he probably was no wiser for his efforts.

We traveled on swiftly through Ramleh. Mr. Nir explained that we were going to Jaffa Port. As in the office at the prison there was nothing else to talk about as we journeyed but of the strange events of the night. There was no longer need for security for the prisoner, and this in itself loosened tongues and revealed information not heretofore made public.

There was a faint hint of light in the sky as we approached the port at about 3:45 A.M. I remarked that it was here that I had landed when we first arrived in 1935. Then our ship had anchored far offshore and we had come ashore in lighters.

At the gate of the port a port policeman was waiting on a bicycle to guide us to where a small tender was waiting. Another car joined us there on the dock, adding four to our party. Our party now consisted of Mr. Nir, the Ramleh district officer, the police officer representing the police section (the one who had been with us in the prison office where we noticed his tattooed numbers from the concentration camp), a prison secretary, who had arranged the forms for us to sign, two other prison officials, and myself.

We stood on the open deck while the boat slowly chugged out through the rocks by the breakwater and headed for a police patrol boat a mile or more away in the open sea. There was quite a swell, and in order to board the patrol boat, when we reached it, one had to wait until the two boats were level, then properly gauge the distance, and jump. Fortunately none missed.

At first it was indicated for us to make our way to the stern. A metal step protruded near the engine-room door and I bruised my shin on it. It was probably the last hurt Adolf Eichmann caused humanity. I carried the scar for some time.

Later the captain invited us to the forward saloon where we sat around the table and were served very hot coffee. Our boat was now headed out to sea, the shore line gradually being swallowed up in the mist. The captain informed us that we were sailing to the boundary of Israel territorial water, six miles offshore.

The time passed quickly and before long Mr. Nir called me to come. We all made our way aft to the stern.

Solemnly Mr. Nir uncovered the tin containing the earthly remains of Adolf Eichmann. We stood by the rail as the tin was upturned. It was 4:35 A.M. Into the swirling waters at the stern he slowly poured the ashes. They rested but a moment on the foam-colored water washed up under the stern and then sank from view.

I had been told not to conduct any special service, as the ashes were consigned to the ocean. I bowed my head in silent prayer. *"Earth to earth, ashes to ashes, dust to dust. May God have mercy on his soul. May God comfort the bereaved ones, both of his family and those whom he had caused to be bereaved. Amen."* What more could I say for this man who had attained world notoriety as one of history's most monstrous assassins? He had one of the fairest trials in history. He had rejected the gospel of Jesus Christ. When told of salvation through Him Who had died for him—even for an Adolf Eichmann—he boldly claimed that he needed no mediator, no savior.

What could one pray for such a man, unrepentant of sin and unwilling to believe? *May God have mercy on his soul.*

Mr. Nir rinsed the pail with sea water and emptied it into the ocean. Slowly the ship circled back toward shore. There was no other ship in sight and the shore line was not visible. There, alone in the sea, the ashes of Adolf Eichmann slowly sank into the depths of the Mediterranean to await the resurrection morn which John so graphically described as he had seen in his Apocalyptic vision and recorded in the twentieth chapter of the Book of Revelation: *And I saw a great white throne, and him that sat on it, from whose face the earth and the heaven fled away; and there was found no place for* them. And I saw the dead, small and great, stand before God; and the books were opened; and another book was opened, which is the book of life: and the dead were judged out of those things which were written in the books, according to their works. And the sea gave up the dead which were in it; and death and hell delivered up the dead which were in them; and they were judged every man according to their works. And death and hell were cast into the lake of fire. This is the second death. And whosoever was not found written in the book of life was cast into the lake of fire.

APPENDIX

Chronology of Sessions at Ramleh Prison between Rev. and Mrs. William L. Hull and Adolf Eichmann

Session	1	Wednesday,	April	11, 1962	10:00 A.M.
Session	2	Friday,	April	20, 1962	10:00 A.M.
Session	3	Thursday,	April	26, 1962	10:00 A.M.
Session	4	Sunday,	April	29, 1962	10:00 A.M.
Session	5	Wednesday,	May	2, 1962	10:00 A.M.
Session	6	Monday,	May	7, 1962	10:00 A.M.
Session	7	Thursday,	May	10, 1962	10:00 A.M.
Session	8	Sunday,	May	13, 1962	10:00 A.M.
Session	9	Wednesday,	May	16, 1962	10:00 A.M.
Session	10	Sunday,	May	20, 1962	10:00 A.M.
Session	11	Tuesday,	May	22, 1962	3:00 P.M.
Session	12	Thursday,	May	24, 1962	11:00 A.M.
Session	13	Thursday,	May	31, 1962	10:00 A.M.
Session	14	Thursday,	May	31, 1962	11:20 P.M.

All sessions lasted approximately one hour except the April 11th and May 13th sessions, which were shorter. The last session just preceding the execution lasted for twenty-five minutes.

Planned Order of Spiritual Subjects
for Ministering to Adolf Eichmann

1. God's judgment versus man's.
2. All have sinned.
3. All are lost because of sin.
4. Christ died for sinners.
5. All can be saved.
6. Salvation is through faith.

7. Faith is a gift of God.
8. Jesus is coming again—resurrection of dead and living.

Scriptures used at each session at Ramleh Prison (either discussed with Adolf Eichmann or a list left with him to study):

SESSION 1 Luke 12:4–5
Ecclesiastes 12:14
Hebrews 9:27
Psalms 9:17
Jude 13
Matthew 11:20–24
Psalms 37:27–28; 37–38
Matthew 7:13–14

SESSION 2 Romans 3:23
John 3:16
Ecclesiastes 7:20
Jeremiah 17:9–10
Romans 3:10
Isaiah 64:6

SESSION 3 John 3:1–21, especially 3–6, 17–18
Luke 13:1–3
Luke 12:1–5
Proverbs 14:12
John 14:6
Psalms 1:1–6

SESSION 4 Romans 1:16–32, especially verse 20
Proverbs 14:12
John 14:6
Ezekiel 18:4
John 3:3
Hebrews 9:27
John 8:31–32
John 3:3–6
John 3:17–18

SESSION 5 Romans 3:10, 23
Ezekiel 18:27

Leviticus 17:11
Isaiah 53:3–6
Genesis 22:1–14, especially verse 8
John 8:56–58
Romans 4:3
Matthew 1:20–21
John 1:29
John 10:17–18
Matthew 20:17–19
John 19:16–18, 30
Romans 5:8
1 Peter 2:24

SESSION 6 Luke 15:11–32

SESSION 7 Psalms 25:14
John 10:1–9
John 12:44–49
John 14:1–27
Mark 16:16
John 20:31
2 Thessalonians 2:10–11
John 3:16
2 Corinthians 4:3–6

SESSION 8 No scriptures used

SESSION 9 Scripture booklet in German,
Published by Scripture Gift Mission,
London, England.
English title, *Daily Strength*

SESSION 10 A Bible study on *The Promised Christ*
Genesis 3:15
Virgin birth, suffering, victory

Genesis 4:3–5
The necessity of a "blood" sacrifice

Genesis 22:7–8 (verses 1–14)
The drama of the substitutionary sacrifice

Exodus 12:3–13
The lamb was a type of Christ

Leviticus 1:1–4
Faith in action

Leviticus 17:11
God's positive promise

Psalms 2:6–7
God's Son promised

Isaiah 7:14
Messiah to be virgin-born

Isaiah 9:6
Messiah to be the Mighty God

Isaiah 53
Prophetic picture of suffering of Christ

Isaiah 1:18
God's invitation

Ezekiel 33:11
Why will you die?
  You will die if you do not believe
  John 8:24
  You will live if you believe
  John 11:25–26; 3:14–18, 36; 4:13–14; 5:24
Scripture booklet in German,
Published by Scripture Gift Mission,
London, England.
English title, *The Upward Way*

SESSION 11   No scripture verses used

SESSION 12   No scripture verses used

SESSION 13   The following verses were prepared for reading and study but Eichmann refused to read in his Bible:

Isaiah 55:6–7
Matthew 28:18

John 8:19–24
Ephesians 2:8–9
Romans 10:9–10
Luke 23:39–43

<small>SESSION</small> 14   No scripture verses used